Psychology, Crime, and Justice Series

COP WATCH

Spectators, Social Media, and Police Reform

HANS TOCH

American Psychological Association • *Washington, DC*

Published by
American Psychological Association
750 First Street, NE
Washington, DC 20002
www.apa.org

To order
APA Order Department
P.O. Box 92984
Washington, DC 20090-2984
Tel: (800) 374-2721; Direct: (202) 336-5510
Fax: (202) 336-5502; TDD/TTY: (202) 336-6123
Online: www.apa.org/pubs/books
E-mail: order@apa.org

In the U.K., Europe, Africa, and the Middle East, copies may be ordered from
American Psychological Association
3 Henrietta Street
Covent Garden, London
WC2E 8LU England

Typeset in Minion by Circle Graphics, Inc., Columbia, MD

Printer: The Maple-Vail Book Manufacturing Group, York, PA
Cover Designer: Naylor Design, Washington, DC

The opinions and statements published are the responsibility of the authors, and such opinions and statements do not necessarily represent the policies of the American Psychological Association.

Library of Congress Cataloging-in-Publication Data

Toch, Hans.
 Cop watch : spectators, social media, and police reform / Hans Toch.
    p. cm.
 Includes bibliographical references and index.
 ISBN-13: 978-1-4338-1119-7 (alk. paper)
 ISBN-10: 1-4338-1119-7 (alk. paper)
 1. Police—United States. 2. Police brutality—United States. 3. Police-community relations—United States. I. Title.
 HV8139.T63 2012
 363.20973—dc23
                                    2011039010

British Library Cataloguing-in-Publication Data
A CIP record is available from the British Library.

Printed in the United States of America
First Edition

DOI: 10.1037/13618-000

To the memory of Vincent O'Leary

An inspiring president, a supportive dean,
a loyal colleague, and a good friend.

Contents

Foreword

Shadd Maruna

In my all-time favorite essay on pedagogy, titled "Falling in Love with a Book," Hans Toch (1990) argued that there is a difference between recognizing that a book is good and being swept off one's feet: "The former can be a judgment; the latter is an experience" (p. 248). For me, reading a Hans Toch book is always an experience, and editing this one certainly swept me off my feet, to say the least.

Because this important new work is the second title in my new American Psychological Association (APA) book series, "Psychology, Crime, and Justice," it is my great privilege to open the book with a few remarks. In fact, this is an honor for which I have waited a decade now. In 2001, Toch wrote the foreword for my own APA book, *Making Good: How Ex-Convicts Reform and Rebuild Their Lives.* As a junior scholar and a first-time author, I made sure that the APA put his name on the front cover of the book and even suggested that "with a foreword by Hans Toch" be written in bolder font than my own name. This schoolboy trick worked wonders: For years, the bookseller Amazon.com accidentally advertised the book as "*Making Good* by Hans Toch," which surely accounts for 90% of its sales. My only complaint was the number of people (my mother included) who told me that the foreword was their favorite part of the book.

There will be no such stealing of the spotlight here. *Cop Watch* is quintessentially and inimitably Tochian; no one else could have written it. That said, some of the content of this book—in particular, the emphasis in the second half on the role of the "new media" in shaping police–community interactions—may come as something of a surprise to those who know the author personally. There is something wonderfully ironic about a confirmed Luddite, who only recently joined the world of e-mail, writing with such insight about the influence of Internet-based social networking, cellular phone technology, and citizen blogging on police–community relationships.

Yet, as new as these developments are, the issues Toch tackles herein have been long-standing concerns of his 50-year project in social psychology. Most obviously, the book returns to the pioneering research by Toch and his colleagues J. Douglas Grant and Raymond T. Galvin exploring the role of police as "problem solvers" (1975; see also Toch, 1992; Toch & Grant, 2005). This phenomenon, first identified by Toch and his colleagues in the late 1960s, was eventually given the name "problem-oriented policing," which then begat "community policing" and "broken-windows policing" and the endless graduate theses breathlessly exploring these "new" innovations in the subsequent decades.

Indeed, this book begins with a return to some of the actual data collected by Toch and colleagues during this tumultuous transition in policing history. This fascinating interview material has sat in storage for decades, worn and yellowing from age and cigar smoke. Yet, these previously unpublished findings have a surprising resonance for contemporary policing issues, as Toch demonstrates in the second half of his elegant argument.

Most intriguingly, though, the book represents Toch's return to even deeper, more personal roots—his PhD work at Princeton in social psychology. As a founding member of the State University of New York at Albany's School of Criminal Justice (the first PhD-granting program in criminal justice in the United States), Hans Toch's name today is synonymous with applied research on policing and prisons. Yet, his first love was actually the study of the crowd, and his first publications in the early 1950s were in the journal *Public Opinion Quarterly*. Toch describes these beginnings with his trademark wit and humility:

> When I arrived at Princeton as an impecunious grad student, they assigned me a sinecure at the Office of Public Opinion Research, which then consisted of myself and a secretary. (The secretary was

x

better looking than I was.) The first course I ever taught was "Public Opinion and Propaganda"—an extension course for UCLA [University of California, Los Angeles]-San Diego. A shipmate[1]—Robert Parvin—had to sign up so that I could meet minimum registration requirements. (H. Toch, personal communication, July 29, 2011)

Humble origins or not, Toch wrote the groundbreaking *Social Psychology of Social Movements* in 1965, and in 1969, he coauthored the chapter "Collective Behavior: Crowds and Social Movements" for the *Handbook of Social Psychology*, with no less a figure than Stanley Milgram. Yet, when Toch found himself—he says mostly "by accident"—becoming one of the founding figures of academic criminal justice studies, he got distracted from this wider project on collectivities and crowds. In some ways, then, the present volume can be read as Toch's homecoming, four decades later, and a reconciliation of these two discrete halves of his extraordinary career. (Besides showing an impressive persistence, there is also something wonderful for those of us teaching and supervising graduate students to think that 50 years hence they might still be wrestling with the questions raised in all of these seminars and tutorials.)

Toch achieves this reconciliation by calling attention to the role of a group of ubiquitous but heretofore-invisible actors in the policing process. In policing research, our criminological lens is typically focused either on the arrestees or the arresters. Like a drama, we focus on the protagonist and antagonist, the hero and the villain (and the police can be easily cast in either role). Occasionally, policing research also focuses on the wider audience of the play—measuring community "satisfaction" with or "approval" of policing, or perceptions of police legitimacy among the wider public. Do we cheer the police or boo them? All are important aspects of understanding policing.

Yet, for the first time, in this work Toch focuses his lens instead on a different but equally important group of players. Never lost for eloquent metaphors, Toch calls them "the clamorous chorus," comparing their role with the role played by the chorus in classic Greek tragedies. They are not

---

[1]Toch served in the navy during the Korean War—heroically and "single-handedly" protecting San Diego from attack (H. Toch, personal communications, September 1998 through August 2001).

the key participants in the drama of arrest and prosecution, but neither are they passive audience members. They are bystanders who all but insert themselves into the action and actively influence the outcomes in important, if indirect, ways. In particular, they act as interpreters and opinion leaders for the wider audience, helping "the community" or "the general public" decide when to cheer and when to boo.

This is a powerful role, made obvious by the efforts of the police to silence them—confiscating cellular phones and digital cameras, arresting noisy citizens for obstructing the course of justice, or simply ordering such cop watchers to "move along" and "mind their own business." Policing, after all, is fundamentally performative in nature, as expressive as it is instrumental, with its shows of strength, routine patrols, and symbolic arrests intended not just to solve crimes but also to inspire public confidence that the state is "in charge." And no good performer wants to have to put up with a Greek chorus standing on the sidelines questioning and reinterpreting the proceedings, challenging the official script, emboldening the antagonist, and redirecting the action. Such intervention is particularly unwelcome when one is trying to play the hero but the chorus insists on recasting him or her as villain.

With this research, Toch allows the police to talk back to the clamorous chorus, giving their perspective on these emotional dynamics. With the benefit of hindsight, we can see how these interactions—far from perverting the course of justice—were themselves fundamental in the reform of policing and the development of new strategies for building police legitimacy developed in the past 4 decades. This history is far from over, however, and in the second half of Toch's book, we see that the clamorous chorus has hardly gone away either. Indeed, changes in communication technology have given the chorus an even louder megaphone for interpreting and directing the action. These developments may have as much of an impact on the future of policing as have improvements in DNA and surveillance technology. The message is, in other words, if you want to know where policing will go in the future, listen out for the chorus.

In that regard, of all the choral singers—or cop watchers—in all the world, Hans Toch is surely one of the wisest. The remarkable final chapter of this volume—where Toch goes "clamorous" himself with a withering analysis of the persistent profiling of poor and minority citizens in police stops and searches—reinforces this fact. In his preface, Toch apologizes for ending this fascinating book on such a low note, blaming decades of practice in being a grouch. I disagree. Like the best Greek chorus, Toch is sounding a pitch-perfect warning here to would-be heroes of the police that if they continue to be carried away by an authoritarian hubris, they may find themselves starring in a familiar tragedy involving "the pride that comes before the fall."

REFERENCES

Milgram, S., & Toch, H. (1969). Collective behavior: Crowds and social movements. In G. Lindzey & E. Aronson (Eds.), *The handbook of social psychology* (2nd ed., Vol. 4, pp. 507–610). Reading, MA: Addison-Wesley.

Toch, H. (1965). *The social psychology of social movements.* Indianapolis, IN: Bobbs-Merrill.

Toch, H. (1990). Falling in love with a book. *Journal of Criminal Justice Education, 1*, 245–254.

Toch, H. (1992). *Violent men: An inquiry into the psychology of violence* (Rev. ed.). Washington, DC: American Psychological Association.

Toch, H., & Grant, J. D. (2005). *Police as problem solvers: How frontline workers can promote organizational and community change* (2nd ed.). Washington, DC: American Psychological Association.

Toch, H., Grant, J. D., & Galvin, R. T. (1975). *Agents of change: A study in police reform.* Cambridge, MA: Schenkman Books.

Preface

The chief protagonist of one of Molière's plays explained that he was surprised and gratified when someone reliably assured him that he knew how to speak prose. At this juncture in my career, I appear to be in a similarly fortunate position. I had been plugging along, working on what I hoped might become a book, but I have to admit that I had no idea what I might have accomplished once I was done.

It would be difficult to imagine my delight when a reviewer of the penultimate version of my manuscript informed the publisher (the American Psychological Association) that the book has several foci, all of which are of scholarly importance:

- alterations in the role of the new media in amplification of (primarily) negative views of policing;
- changes in the sources that shaped public opinion in the last 30 years;
- changes in policing and the views of the police and their craft in this same period;
- alterations in the police occupational culture and public political activities of police spokespersons;
- changes in the role of police and policing in the "high politics" of the city—in this case, Seattle, Washington;
- changes in police leadership and presentational rhetoric in recent years.

This listing sounded impressive to me, and I was proud to be associated with it. However, I had the lingering suspicion that if I had approximated any of these goals, I would not be entitled to claim credit for it. Deep down inside I knew that I had not shaped this book—the book shaped itself, like the proverbial amoeba, acquiring its exotic configuration, including squishy tentacles, on its own. The initial idea had been vague, but modest: to try for a recapitulation exercise, an attempt to revisit some of my past applied encounters and the settings in which these had taken place. What would a nice psychologist like me be doing working with offenders or with cops? And what would nice cops be doing working with a psychologist like me? These were the kind of retrospective questions that appeared suitable for an academic in his rapidly declining years.

My scheme for writing a thinly disguised memoir was fortunately aborted early in the game. I had been plowing through old interview transcripts to jog my moribund memory—specifically, to evoke recollections relating to some violence-related research (Toch, 1969)—when I made a serendipitous discovery. I began noticing some passages in the narratives that had been shared with me by police officers that I had not attended to before. The officers were reminiscing about some of their more memorable experiences on the street, and several of them alluded to bystanders who had interfered with their work. The significance of these bystander interpolations was apparent to the officers, but it did not register with me, despite the embarrassing fact that the solid scholarly literature at my disposal should have alerted me to the importance of these observations—bystanders were objecting to police actions and police officers were taking notice. In retrospect, it is now clear to me that I was so single-mindedly entranced by unfolding police–citizen confrontations that I did not care to be sidetracked by the ancillary behavior of anybody else. The play was the thing, so who cared about the chorus?

The officers I was talking with 5 decades ago in what I now call "West Coast City" complained about what they saw as unfriendly attention—and sometimes, hostile interference—from spectators to their work. The officers told me that they had felt sufficiently strongly about the unwelcome nature of these interpositions that they recalled allowing themselves to be distracted by them, sometimes being deflected from their initial designs and provoked to take retaliatory action. I did not realize at the time (though the officers obviously did) that spectators not only exerted a significant impact on the encounters that they had been witnessing but also elevated their importance by endowing them with political significance. The officers also intuited that the sentiments expressed by some of their antagonistic spectators reflected prevalent reservations in the community about the way police work was being conducted.

The officers did not go on to conclude that abrasive police interventions in minority neighborhoods—hit-and-run action that had provided them with a tangible sense of accomplishment—might be inviting the bad feelings they were encountering among members of the public. The fact that the officers did not draw this connection is in retrospect hardly surprising because they were doing their work as they had always assumed police work should be done—and as they were sure the public thought police work should be done. The leaders of the police profession, however, did not have the luxury to stick to those guns. The more thoughtful police executives during the period—and these prominently included the head of the organization with which my informants were affiliated—had begun to embark on a process of reform, designed to fundamentally reshape the approach to policing of their departments to enhance its community acceptance.

This resolve to change the way business was conducted not surprisingly invited resentment among many rank-and-file officers who did not see the need for change. For most of the officers, the animosity they had been experiencing in the community was unadulterated subversion or a product of deficient child rearing that produced disrespect for authority. Consequently, once the progressive police chiefs embarked on their community-oriented reforms, the prevailing view in the locker rooms was that these initiatives represented shameless pandering and transparent compromise. As noted by the criminologist Egon Bittner (1980),

> the response to outside conditions came to be viewed by many policemen as a coerced concession to rebellion. These men, who view themselves as custodians of the public order, consider it deplorable to enter into any kind of negotiations with parties that dared to challenge this order. (p. 114)

The juxtaposition of top-down and bottom-up perspectives in police organizations gave rise to some ugly confrontations (which I shall sample in this volume), but the passage of time has resulted in across-the-board accommodations, particularly as police officers have begun to admit that members of the community may have legitimate grievances and that some citizen complaints may deserve careful scrutiny (as long as excruciating due process is extended to the officers who are complained against). I review some of the changes that produced this mellowed ambience later in this book.

The book is concerned with the history of police reform, but the history I am mainly concerned with is that of those bystanders and spectators I did not attend to when they were first brought to my attention. And in that regard, I have to emphasize that an immense amount of change has taken place over the intervening period of 5 or so decades. The fact was recently highlighted by a panel of judges in a decision of a federal court of appeals (*Glik v. Cunniffe*, 2011) which reaffirmed the right of contemporaneous spectators to videotape police–citizen encounters. The judges noted that

> changes in technology and society have made the lines between private citizen and journalist exceedingly hard to draw. The proliferation of electronic devices with video-recording capabilities means that many of our images of current events come from bystanders with ready cell or digital camera . . . and news stories are now just as likely to be broken by a blogger at her computer as a reporter at a major newspaper. (*Glik v. Cunniffe*, 2011, p. 5)

A beneficent consequence delineated by the judges was that "ensuring the public's right to gather information about their officials not only aids in the uncovering of abuses . . . but also may have a salutary effect on the functioning of government more generally" (*Glik v. Cunniffe*, 2011, p. 4).

A police officer who is nowadays engaged in an unseemly confrontation can literally discover him- or herself acting on a public stage. The use of force can be memorialized in vivid color and revealing detail, to be disseminated on the evening news, under morning newspaper headlines, and in a range of outlets over the Internet. Spectator responses to the officer's exploits can eventuate from across the globe, featuring vigorous debate about the substance of the transgressions. Given a series of incidents involving members of the same police departments, systemic questions are apt to be posed about the department as a whole, questions insistently reiterated by activists.

There came a juncture in the exploration of these questions in this book when I needed a change of venue. After mature but shamelessly contaminated deliberation, I opted to focus on a city of which I happen to be a long-term secret admirer and which also happened to have a police department whose efforts to be transparent and responsive I thought had been commendable, even if not uniformly successful.[1] The second portion of this volume has therefore turned into a memento of Seattle, while it records and dissects recent events that involve the city and its police department. Ironically, given my emphasis in the second part of this narrative on the evolving role of technology, I have drawn the documentation for my Seattle account largely from the Internet. What I may or may not have accomplished in the process has been eloquently delineated by my reviewer (see previous), and I find that I have nothing to add.

I was tempted to conclude the book with a few prescriptive ruminations about the process of police reform. But having ventilated my suggestions in that regard on a number of occasions to no discernible effect, I saw no point in repeating myself. Instead, I have decided to end this volume more usefully by pointing to what I think is incontrovertible evidence of retrograde trends in the conduct of police work these days, which appear to inexorably erode public support for the police.

One example of these trends can be found in the response to the recent Occupy Wall Street movement, in which police have employed aggressive tactics against peaceful demonstrators in various cities. The intense media coverage of these events has led Norm Stamper, who was police chief in Seattle during the World Trade Organization protests in

---

[1] A recent example (on both counts) was provided in a report from Seattle published in the *New York Times*, which recorded that "the Police Department in this technology-conscious city had started a 12-hour experiment of posting almost all its emergency calls on Twitter. It wanted citizens to see what a day in the life of the department was really like" (Seelye, 2011, p. A17). The article goes on to announce, "The Police Department will . . . start another experiment next month, with officers in the field sending out Twitter messages of what they did on their calls only, of course, after they have resolved the incident" (Seelye, 2011, p. A17). A move of this kind could be designed to preempt some of the spectator involvement I discuss in this volume.

November 1999, to think about the relevance of his experience to these more recent confrontations. The target of protesters in 1999 was globalization, as represented by the World Trade Organization, which was meeting—or was attempting to meet—in the Seattle Convention Center. The police response to this demonstration involved the extensive use of tear gas, which contributed to an escalating confrontation, which in turn culminated in a seriously disruptive riot.

Stamper, who had been hired as a community-oriented reformer in 1994 but lost his job in the wake of the disturbance, thinks back to the morning in Seattle in which "large contingents of demonstrators began to converge at a key downtown intersection" and "sat down and refused to budge" (Stamper, 2011, p. 6). Stamper recalls that he responded to demands that he have the protesters removed from the premises, which (succinctly summarized) "caused all hell to break loose." Stamper reflects in retrospect that "the 'Battle in Seattle' . . . was a huge setback—for the protesters, my cops, the community" (p. 7). He now adds that

> more than a decade later, the police response to the Occupy move-
> ment . . . brings into sharp relief the acute and chronic problems of
> American law enforcement. Seattle might have served as a cautionary
> tale, but instead, US police forces have become increasingly milita-
> rized, and it's showing in cities everywhere: the NYPD "white shirt"
> coating innocent people with pepper spray, arrests of two student
> journalists at Occupy Atlanta, the declaration of public property as
> off-limits and the arrests of protesters for "trespassing."

Stamper (2011) concludes that

> the paramilitary bureaucracy [of police departments] and the cul-
> ture it engenders—a black-and-white world in which police unions
> serve above all to protect the brotherhood—is worse today than it
> was in the 1990s. Such agencies inevitably view protesters as the
> enemy. And young people, poor people and people of color will for-
> ever experience the institution as an abusive, military force—not just
> during demonstrations but every day, in neighborhoods throughout
> the country (ibid.).

Despite such misgivings, Stamper has envisaged a direction for what he sees as overdue reform, which in his words might include "building a progressive police organization, created by rank-and-file officers, civilian employees, and community representatives" in which "cops and citizens would forge an authentic partnership in policing the city."

Chief Stamper is in a unique position to appreciate the dilemma posed for the police by groups of peaceful demonstrators who appear determined to congregate in public places. But Chief Stamper is in an even more unique position to appreciate the drawback of responding to demonstrators in what he calls a "militaristic" fashion. Today, the harmful consequences he alludes to can be even more serious than they were ten years ago. Today's consequences follow from the instantaneous and widespread dissemination of scenarios such as that of a group of kneeling women casually sprayed with chemical irritants, or of a veteran injured with a tear-gas canister grenade, or of reporters beaten in the course of being inappropriately arrested. Such scenarios raise fundamental questions around the globe about the role of police forces in a civil society.

I would have liked to end on a happier note, but after eight decades of being a grouch, I cannot afford to tarnish my reputation.

Acknowledgments

For a person who considers writing a book, there is nothing more important than finding a congenial and nurturing publisher. I have been blessed in this regard and should like to take this opportunity to thank American Psychological Association (APA) Books and Mary Lynn Skutley, to whom I have been indebted for 20 years of unswerving confidence, collaboration, and friendship. Mary Lynn's faith was most recently tested as she was presented with a project so vague that for most of its lifetime it could have been alluded to as "the book without a name." As Mary Lynn's culminating contribution to this cause, she supplied the pithy title for our book, and a subtitle.

My development editor was Tyler Aune, whose assignment was to goad an author celebrated for his pigheadedness and rigidity into considering entertaining some bare-minimal revisions. To make Tyler's unenviable task even less inviting, he discovered along the way that he had to guide his superannuated charge through the rudiments and the mechanics of editing. Throughout, Tyler exercised both patience and wisdom, and unfailing good humor. I thank him and forgive him the short vacation he took while editing the book, in contravention to my instructions.

I should particularly like to recognize the contribution of my valued friend and colleague Shadd Maruna, under whose auspices (as APA series editor) this book will appear. Maruna's exalted role provides him with the prerogative of writing a foreword, which will convert my contribution into an extended appendix. I shall forgive Shadd Maruna for upstaging me, because he has been a consistent source of good ideas. On comparable grounds, I should like to thank Jay Wachtel, who started life as my student but has lately functioned as my teacher.

The writing of this book has been made possible by the fact that my long-time employers, the University at Albany (State University of New York), did not summarily evict me following my retirement. For this, I am grateful.

Lastly, the peer-review process offers ironclad confidentiality, and I have therefore been prevented from identifying the reviewers of my manuscript. But strictly on the grounds that if it walks like a duck and quacks like a duck, it may be a duck, I should like to express my warm appreciation to Peter Manning.

ONE

WEST COAST CITY, 1967–1971

1

The Clamorous Chorus

Encounters between police officers and citizens are apt to take place on the streets—and thus they often occur in the presence of spectators who are either already present on the scene or who become attracted to the situation as it unfolds. These spectators can elect to remain passive or decide to play a more active role—hopefully, one short of participation in the confrontation itself.

Under ideal circumstances, police officers can discharge their obligations in public encounters to the satisfaction of the citizens with whom they are dealing and can thus earn the admiration of spectators who appreciate the professionalism of their conduct and the happy resolutions they are able to achieve. Such outcomes would constitute successful performances as defined by the dramaturgical perspective, according to which "the police are dramatic actors, [who] must wrestle collectively and individually with the salient dramatic dilemmas of their role and occupation" (Manning, 1977, p. 17). In performances thus defined, the spectators play a crucial supporting role. Goffman (1959) thus pointed out the following:

> It has been argued that the audience contributes in a significant way to the maintenance of a show by exercising tact or protective practices on behalf of the performers. It is apparent that if the audience is to employ tact on the performer's behalf, the performer must act in such a way as to make the rendering of this assistance possible. This will require discipline and circumspection. (p. 234)

Where there are lapses in "discipline and circumspection" and performances begin to become unconvincing, spectators can prove helpful to performers by providing corrective feedback, to which the performers must be receptive. Goffman (1959) wrote,

> The performer must be sensitive to hints and ready to take them, for it is through hints that the audience can warn the performer that his show is unacceptable and that he had better modify it quickly if the situation is to be saved. (p. 234)

THE CONTRIBUTION OF SPECTATORS TO POLICE ENCOUNTERS

The involvement of spectators in police–citizen confrontations invites comparison with the role played by the chorus in classic Greek tragedies. The chorus has been called the "moral barometer of the play in classical Greek theatre" because chorus members "constantly offered opinions on wickedness, punishment, and righteousness" (Maria, 2004, para. 7). The chorus asked questions of the actors, gave unsolicited advice (which was frequently ignored), and provided support to protagonists by supplying vividly partisan testimony. Through harsh and grating songs, it advertised and amplified the action, converting private encounters into public conflicts. One authority on the subject noted:

> The chorus . . . wailed aloud its grief, and sympathized with the woe of the puppets of the gods. . . . It was the ideal spectator, the soul of being purged, as Aristotle expressed it, by Pity and Fear,

flinging its song and its cry among the passions and pain of others.
(Watt, 1908, p. 15)

(Choruses volubly accentuated the emotions of protagonists but stopped short of intervening in the plot. The parallel would thus no longer apply to spectators who become riot participants.)

Passive spectators are best described as *bystanders* because their contribution consists of "standing by" while the scenario unfolds. That does not mean that bystanders have no measurable impact. Bystanders can affect the outcome of confrontations when one or both of the contending parties become aware of their availability as witnesses and modify their behavior to take this fact into account.[1] Given a police officer's cognizance of available bystanders, for example, the officer may effectuate an arrest for an offense he might otherwise overlook, whereas his opponent might stage a spectacular show of resistance to garner admiration from his or her bystanding peers.

In this book, my interest lies in examining the contribution of active spectators to police–citizen encounters—particularly in the response of spectators to incidents that appear to have degenerated, in the sense that officers are being perceived as using excessive force. In these controversial encounters, spectators can play the amplification role of the partisan chorus: converting local confrontations into public conflicts that have a dramatic impact and carry consequences.

In the first part of the book, I focus on incidents that occurred in the late sixties in a racially divided metropolitan area (which I call "West Coast City") that epitomized the storms and stresses of the period. In this highly polarized setting, the chorus's contribution to police encounters was particularly consequential because it dramatized prevailing race-related conflicts, underlined the urgency of the problem, and thus helped to instigate one of the first and most radical among the avalanche of police-community-relations–centered reform efforts that swept the country in the 1960s and

---

[1] We shall see in Part II of this book that the introduction of cell phones and digital cameras substantially enhanced the contribution of bystanders beyond any impact that the awareness of their presence might have had on police and citizen participants (particularly those of scenarios of the unbridled use of physical force) and could serve to instigate organizational change, facilitate legal recourse, inspire second-generation chorus participation, and sometimes contribute to the start of riots.

1970s. My focus is on the role of the chorus in the escalation of specific incidents—including the way citizens (and occasionally, the officers) recruited passive bystanders into becoming actively participating spectators.

A BACKDROP OF COLLECTIVE RESENTMENT

Wildly successful efforts to "mobilize a chorus" were being staged with increasing frequency in the 1960s—particularly in minority neighborhoods, where choruses were also assiduously and speedily self-mobilized. These developments suggested that many of the citizens who were witnessing police–citizen encounters had strong preexisting misgivings about the police that predisposed them to choral membership. Ironically, this prevalent hostility toward the police was most in evidence in cities in which police departments had prided themselves on being "professional," because in practice this meant embarking on no-holds-barred, full-throated arrest-centered enforcement as a matter of premeditated policy. In these communities, police officers who were out on patrol had come to be widely perceived as—and had learned to perceive themselves as—members of occupying forces embarked on "search-and-destroy" expeditions.[2]

THE PSYCHOLOGY OF CROWDS

In the face of widespread hostilities and their expression during daily encounters with citizens, police officers on the streets could not avoid the realization that as a first step they had to somehow accommodate what William Muir (1977) called "the psychology of crowds," though there were many officers at the time who were slow to learn the lesson and a few who as a matter of course instigated choral membership among hostile citizens by being patronizing and domineering. Muir thus observed:

> [One officer] would come on with an ultimatum, uttered loudly and publicly to antagonist and crowds alike. "You're supposed to act like

---

[2] In Chapter 10, I examine the degree to which this pattern appears to have survived the evolution of policing and continues to present problems.

normal human beings. Right? Well, you're not doing it, and we've been here time and time again. We've been trying to teach you people how to get with each other. But the next time I'll take the whole stinking lot of you to jail. You people can't get along. And it'll cost you $100 a head to get out of jail." (p. 103)

Muir (1977) also observed officer behavior that was seemingly calculated to invite resentment through blatantly insensitive across-the-board and indiscriminate enforcement. To not provoke or encourage antagonistic reactions, Muir posited that officers of the period had to become attuned to the psychology of crowd formation:

> [An effective police officer] had to understand what a difference a crowd made. Neighbors involved in fighting each other behaved differently in front of a crowd than in privacy. The policeman had to understand that neighborhood reputations for indomitability were on the line. . . . A policeman who could successfully lower those expectations was taking a crucial step toward closing the gap between an honorable performance (i.e., one which saved face for the neighbor) and a lawful performance (i.e., one which the policeman desired). (p. 105)

Crowd formation and the risk of rioting it implied remained live concerns through the 1960s and 1970s. Officers in both decades had to continue to negotiate volatile situations, which meant that they had to take resentment and opposition in stride and react to spectators' intemperate vocalizations with a measure of equanimity and humor. This challenge remained particularly acute when groups of unemployed young people were forced to spend their time congregated on street corners, hoping for stimulating diversions provided by physical confrontations.

CATALYTIC POLICE INTERVENTIONS

Most degenerating confrontations were initiated by the proactive involvement of officers—by discretionary, on-view interventions—that were targeted at some behavior on the part of citizens that the officers judged to be offensive. These exercises of police discretion almost reliably invited critical reappraisals by ill-disposed members of the chorus. Albert Reiss (1971) thus reported in his seminal study of police behavior (which was conducted in the early and mid-sixties):

> When the police enter a situation on their own initiative, bystanders are more likely to question the legitimacy of their intervention and, therefore, respond with hostility. This is especially true when they intervene in public settings where consensual support for police intervention is low. (p. 145)

Reiss (1971) pointed out that the import of his observation was not that officers ought to have been instructed to withhold police action if and when their interventions were appropriate but that the appropriateness of intervening needed to be established and conveyed to resistant or suspicious citizens:

> The necessity to intervene in the affairs of citizens when coupled with a dependence upon citizen willingness to grant legitimacy to that intervention creates a special problem for the exercise of police authority. The police must *establish their right to intervene* when legitimacy is not granted. (p. 177, emphasis in the original)

In other words, the police were on notice that policing had to somehow regain its street credibility.

A SENSE OF RECIPROCAL ALIENATION

The sixties were a period during which a sense of reciprocal alienation distanced the police from the community and—volubly and acrimoniously—the community from the police. In this climate, each new degenerating confrontation added to the rapidly accumulating reservoir of hostility and resentment. The awareness and documentation of this escalation made the sixties and seventies a disequilibrating and unsettling time in the history of policing. Conference transcripts and commission reports show that it had become obvious to enlightened police administrators that serious rethinking had to be done to counter the fact that so much of the public had lost confidence in the operation of law enforcement (President's Commission on Law Enforcement and the Administration of Justice, 1967).

The most authoritative diagnosis of the crisis that the police profession faced during this period was included in the report of the National Advisory Commission on Civil Disorders (1968), which was known as the Kerner Commission. This commission—a professionally staffed, generously endowed, impeccably nonpartisan enterprise—owed its inception to alarm and concern about the outbreaks of extreme rage and destructiveness that had consecutively—and sometimes concurrently—occurred during the first half of the decade. Fortuitously, the date on which the commission issued its findings coincided with that of yet another bloody disturbance, this time in the nation's capital. This 1968 riot was sparked by the assassination of Martin Luther King, who had dedicated his life to discouraging manifestations of collective violence.

The Kerner Commission pointed out the following in its 1968 report:

> In virtually every case a single "triggering" or "precipitating" incident can be identified as having immediately preceded—within a few hours and in generally the same location—the outbreak of disorder. But this incident was usually a relatively minor, even trivial one, by itself substantially disproportionate to the scale of violence that followed. Often it was an incident of a type which had occurred frequently in the same community in the past without provoking violence. (p. 68)

Interventions by the police frequently formed part of the precipitating incident, and the chorus became the intervening variable in triggering the response. The commission noted the following:

> The final incident . . . and the violence itself, generally occurred at a time and place in which it was normal for many people to be on the streets. In most of the 24 disorders, groups generally estimated at 50 or more persons were on the street at the time and place of the first outbreak. (National Advisory Commission on Civil Disorders, 1968, p. 71)

Tom Wicker (1968), who introduced the commission's report, wrote, "This report is a picture of one nation, divided" (p. v). Hubert Locke (1996), who analyzed and discussed the crisis of confidence in the police that had become a matter of concern for police executives at the time, illustrated its magnitude with a contemporary quote from officials of the National Association for the Advancement of Colored People:

> At present, large numbers (majorities, in some instances) of Negroes have come to regard policemen as oppressors. . . . Finally, it is clear that no police force, operating under conditions short of a police state, can hope to function effectively for very long in a situation of crisis deriving from resentment or resistance on the part of massive proportions of the community in which it works. (Stahl et al., 1966, p. 169, as cited in Locke, 1996, p. 131)

The attribution of causation is not a zero-sum game: Riots were the imminent hypothetical outcome of all degenerating confrontations of this period, and there is no perceptible line that divided incident participants from riot initiators. Thus, a Watts riot participant was quoted as follows:

> Maybe the people of Beverly Hills would riot too if they spent most of their life with a cop's club in their face. Or if they had to get out of an automobile with their hands over their heads to be questioned for doing nothing at all. We're not safe from police brutality even in our own home. (Milgram & Toch, 1969, p. 574)

The Watts riot itself began with a clumsily enacted arrest in the presence of a chorus:

> The suspect [being arrested] resisted, in the presence of a rapidly expanding crowd of spectators. In the face of the crowd's apparent hostility, the officer produced his pistol and called for another car to assist him. He then drove away with the young man and with the latter's mother and brother, both of whom he had arrested. The officer forced the suspect into his patrol car in the presence of the assembled witnesses; he allegedly used a nightstick to prod the young man into

submission. One member of the crowd later declared: "When that happened, all the people standing around got mad." (Milgram & Toch, 1969, p. 571)

The member of the crowd alluded to here hypothesized the genesis of the chorus.

THE CONTRIBUTION OF THE POLICE TO THE PRECIPITATION OF RIOTS

A 1965 governor's commission looking into the police role during the period leading up to and following the Watts riot noted the following:

> An examination of seven riots in northern cities of the United States in 1964 reveals that each one was started over a police incident. . . . In each of the 1964 riots, "police brutality" was an issue, as it was here, and, indeed, as it has been in riots and insurrections elsewhere in the world. The fact that this charge is repeatedly made must not go unnoticed, for there is a real danger that persistent criticism will reduce and perhaps destroy the effectiveness of law enforcement. (Governor's Commission on the Los Angeles Riots, as cited in Vila & Morris, 1999, p. 177)

Feelings toward the police during the sixties and seventies were unquestionably buttressed by all sorts of frustrations nurtured over the preceding period through a gamut of depriving conditions, including sustained poverty, economic hardship, and festering racial discrimination (National Advisory Commission on Civil Disorders, 1968). However, the immediate provocation tended to include what was widely perceived as a pattern of inflexible, totalistic, indiscriminate, and seemingly disproportionate enforcement favored by self-styled "professional" police executives of the time. The intersection of their policy of heavy-handed enforcement with reflexive, on-the-scene responses to what key protagonists invariably defined as racially targeted interventions of individual officers who lacked adequate justification for intervening sparked and fuelled the conflagrations that enmeshed targets of police action and their peers.

THE INCEPTION OF A PARADIGM SHIFT

Inevitably, police administrators and their superiors were invited to consider the advisability of painful self-reviews, which some engaged in more assiduously than others. On the whole, despite the discomforts experienced by those who were involved in police–citizen incidents or who had to deal with their repercussions, the period became a productive turning point for the history of policing. Painful lessons were digested and assimilated—admittedly under duress—by everyone concerned: chiefs and commissioners, politicians in municipal government, and even the activists in conflict with the police. These lessons began to be transmuted into changes in habit and reorientation of perspectives. The initial result was a new understanding of sorts among leaders of the profession, a new view of the interface between police and community: a "police-community-relations" interface, with a variety of organizational changes designed to promulgate it:

> Police leaders assumed that the solution to problems with minor-
> ity citizens lay in improving relations between police officers and
> minorities by creating human relations or community relations units
> in police departments whose responsibility was a community rela-
> tions program and community relations training for police officers.
> (Reiss, 1985, p. 61)

It subsequently became obvious, however, that

> making significant changes in citizen satisfaction and cooperation
> with police . . . requires substantial reorganization and restructuring
> of who does what to whom, how, when, and where. More fundamental
> transformations are required in organization, recruitment, training, and
> control of behavior in policing if these objectives are to be achieved.
> (Reiss, 1985, p. 62)

The earliest of these developments are sometimes dismissed because their initial impact was seemingly evanescent. They are also sometimes retrospectively defined as public-relations moves made by police admin-istrators who were forced to respond to the evidence that police actions and police approaches had contributed to the genesis of riots.[3] Egon Bittner (1980) thus pointed out the following:

> Though one could probably not show that every effort in this direction had been mounted only after some specific incident of civil strife, there can be no doubt that the undertaking as a whole has been reactive in the sense that it followed external pressure rather than the spontaneous appreciation of the need. There is no strong argument against the police to be built on this observation. After all, they were not the only ones to learn the hard way, nor were they the last ones. (p. 114)

The recognition that riots may have been the wake-up call for police reform makes some sense, but a more comprehensive picture has to take into account the corrosive experience of innumerable messy, ugly, unseemly, and expensive police–citizen confrontations and the rethinking these experiences cumulatively inspired.

THE CHORUS, AS VIEWED FROM THE STAGE

The first part of this book is intended to provide a picture of chorus involvements in police encounters in the sixties. Ideally, it would be useful to have firsthand testimonials from chorus members to get a sense of the frustration and anger that fuelled their involvement and to get a feeling for what they might have expected and what they hoped to accomplish. It would be interesting to know how parochial the goals of these chorus members were and how conscious they might have been of their designated historical role, of the civil rights movement that they exemplified, and of the prevailing concerns they reflected relating to police brutality and racial justice. Unfortunately, we have no firsthand information

---

[3] Other riots had taken place in the summers of 1964 and 1965 in Philadelphia, Rochester, Jersey City, Harlem, and Chicago. These disturbances were not conventional race riots:

> The outbursts occurred in the heart of the Negro ghettos, rather than at the boundaries of the Negro–White neighborhoods. The first man attacked in the Philadelphia outbreak of 1964 was a Negro policeman. Race per se seemed to be less an issue than poverty. (Milgram & Toch, 1969, p. 573)

The Watts riot was almost a midpoint. In the "hot" summer of 1966 it was followed by rioting in 38 cities, including in Atlanta, Chicago, Cleveland, Dayton, Omaha, and San Francisco, and by two major disturbances—in Newark, Detroit—in 1967.

relating to these questions, but we are in a position to ask questions such as how police officers participating in degenerating incidents during this period perceived and defined their own behavior and the challenges they faced. How would the officers describe their experiences with chorus formation, and how did they frame their responses to these experiences?

To shed light on these questions, in Chapters 2 through 4 I draw on transcripts of incident-centered interviews[4] that a team of which I was a member conducted with violence-experienced officers[5] in a police department that was in the process of embarking on serious, comprehensive reform (see Toch, 1969).[6] I also explore the resistance among the officers to these community-oriented reforms, reforms that culminated in a vote of no confidence in their chief (Chapter 5). Given the passage of time since these accounts were collected, it might be inviting to exercise judgmental hindsight in reviewing them, but the behavior and perspectives described in the narratives are best assessed against the backdrop of experiences and perspectives that antedate decades of devoutly professed though far-from-smooth progress in police–community relations.

In the three chapters that follow, I relay the experiences of the officers in their own words, which are occasionally redolent with some of the verbal idiosyncrasies and predilections of the period, not only those of officers but also those of the targeted citizens and spectators they quote, who often expressed their resentments and indignation in pungent and colorful prose. In organizing excerpts from the officers' narratives, I group the material thematically, in terms of different roles played by spectators in the unfolding confrontations. In line with the theatrical "chorus" concept, I group the accounts as sets of *scenarios*—defined not only in the dictionary sense as "an account or synopsis of a projected course of action or events"

---

[4]We conducted 31 incident-centered interviews, and 29 of these contained spontaneous descriptions and discussions of spectator participation in incidents.

[5]Each respondent had been repeatedly involved in arrest situations in which perpetrators had been charged with resisting arrest or assault on an officer. Such arrests suggest that incidents might have degenerated into physical confrontations. In the interviews, the officers were invited to describe incidents as they unfolded and to reflect on their experiences relating to these incidents.

[6]The interviews were conducted by J. Douglas Grant, Raymond T. Galvin, and myself, under the auspices of the police department, with the support and sponsorship of the National Institute of Mental Health (NIMH) Center for the Study of Crime and Delinquency. NIMH also supported reform efforts based on findings from the interviews (see Toch, Grant, & Galvin, 1975, for a description of this intervention).

(Scenario, 1984, p. 1049) but also as "an outline or synopsis of a play" (Scenario, 1984, p. 1049)—in these cases, with the proviso that the "plays" are apt to have distinctly unhappy endings.

The scenarios involving spectator participation in police–citizen confrontations can be subsumed under three thematic headings, reflecting the principal concerns of the choruses of the period:

■ a concern with injustice and unfairness of the police intervention (Chapter 2),
■ a concern with brutality or disproportionality of the police response (Chapter 3), and
■ a concern about discrimination or persecution by the police (Chapter 4, illustrating the mutuality of this concern among citizens and officers).

The grouping of scenarios under categories of concern has to be done with caution and with the understanding that a watertight delineation of human concerns is never, ever possible.

2

The Concern With
the Injustice or Unfairness
of Police Interventions

When police officers initiate encounters with citizens, they are often pretending to embark on clean and uncluttered scenarios, such as the following:

> The officer intercepts a citizen and informs him that he has violated a relatively minor provision of the municipal code. The citizen expresses regret and thanks the officer for bringing the matter to his attention.

The following is an ideal-type escalation of this ideal-type scenario:

> The officer informs the citizen that his offense must be taken seriously and therefore requires that the officer effectuate an arrest. The citizen indicates that he fully understands and is immensely sorry to have put the officer to so much trouble.

If need be, the pretend scenarios of officers can make reluctant provision for quiet, well-behaved spectators, provided they keep a respectful and admiring distance from the officer and his involvements with the citizen.

Needless to say, the scenarios that police encounter in the real world—
and certainly those they encountered in the polarized world of the sixties—
differ appreciably from these ideal-type scenarios. The difference can be
highlighted by considering excerpted narratives of two arrest reports from
the period. The first of these describes a traffic stop of a senior citizen and
his wife:

> [The officer] spotted the suspect's vehicle go through [a] red light.
> [The officer] gave chase and stopped [the] vehicle using red light
> and siren . . . [and] asked the suspect for [his] driver's license. The
> suspect stated, "What are you stopping me for? I'm not speeding."
> [The officer] again asked the suspect for [his] driver's license. The
> suspect stated, "I don't have to show you my license because I haven't
> done anything wrong, and I think this is pretty goddamned ridiculous
> to go stopping people and trying to give tickets during the Christmas
> season." [The officer] informed the suspect that he was required by
> law to submit his license to a police officer upon request, and failure
> to do so shall result in arrest. The suspect then submitted [his] license
> to [the officer] and stated, "Where am I living? In some communist
> country?" Suspect # 2 [the suspect's wife] said, "How long have you
> been a police officer? You are just a snot-nosed brat in a blue jacket."
>
> The suspect reached in my window and grasped my badge, and
> [I] stated, "Git your hands off me!" The suspect then stated, "Oh, yeah,"
> and grabbed my badge trying to rip it off and half pulling [me] out of
> the patrol car. [I] lifted the door handle and kicked open the door,
> knocking the suspect to the ground. While doing this, [I] was attacked
> from behind by Suspect # 2 [wife], who was cuffed immediately.
>
> The suspect's vehicle was parked so that it created a hazard;
> therefore, it was towed.

In the report, the officer wrote that he had witnessed a violation, but
the driver of the car complained that he had been mistakenly charged with
speeding. The irate driver and his irate wife then vented their indignation
and questioned the officer's maturity, integrity, and judgment. According
to the officer, he calmly responded by returning to his own car and initiating the paperwork for his citation. This businesslike response appeared

to increase the resentment of the aggrieved citizen and his supportive wife. A messy and embarrassing confrontation resulted and culminated with the elderly couple being arrested, physically restrained, and transported to jail. Both husband and wife were charged with battery and resisting arrest. There was no mention of a traffic violation.

We interviewed this officer, but he did not specifically refer to his confrontation with the elderly driver and his wife. However, he discussed at length his conception of his role in dealing with traffic transgressors:

> Well, I look at it this way. If I am doing something and I'm wrong, I'm wrong, but if I find that I'm doing something right, then I'm going to follow through on it. If I go up there and I find that this person has been speeding—I clocked them at 45 miles an hour—and all of a sudden he says, "What the hell are you stopping me for, Fuzz? I didn't speed," and all this jazz, I'm not going to say, "Well, maybe I made a mistake," or something else. I wouldn't have stopped him if he hadn't clearly committed a violation.[1]

The officer had not been disposed to be particularly flexible, but the lashing to which he was subjected could only have helped to harden his resolve. According to the officer's report, the conversation rapidly got off on the wrong foot. He did not mention any process of mutual appraisal prior to the point at which acrimonious misunderstandings arose, nor did he describe his initial approach or opening remarks. However, he did indicate in his interview that he approached traffic stops with considerable trepidation, which suggests that he would not have started out by exuding boyish charm:

> Let's face it, you don't know who you are stopping, and too darn many police officers get killed. You know, it might be a routine stop. You might see a fellow that has some kids in the car and you think— you know—like, "Daddy with the kids." He might be a kidnapper.

---

[1] This and other excerpts in this chapter are from incident-centered interviews conducted under the auspices of the police department, with the support and sponsorship of the National Institute of Mental Health Center for the Study of Crime and Delinquency.

You stop and think about these things, you know. You read about it in the paper, and maybe to some people it doesn't impress them, but I don't know—I like to hunt and fish, myself, and I'd like to keep on hunting and fishing.

WHO IS CONDUCTING THE CHORUS?

In a second incident that markedly deviated from ideal-type scenarios, officers attempted to arrest a young man who was a conspicuous member of a group of young people congregated on the street:

> There were approximately 100–150 . . . juveniles milling around the area. The defendant, highly emotional, was standing in the middle of the street, screaming profanities to the [other] juveniles. . . . The defendant was tying up traffic by his presence in the middle of the street. The defendant screamed at the top of his voice that the motherfucking officers would have to fight him to get him out of the middle of the street.[2] The crowd was cheering the defendant as he was displaying his animosity toward the police officers`. . . .
>
> The officers and the defendant wrestled in the middle of the street. The crowd at this time began to throw bottles at the officers. . . . The defendant was finally subdued in the hallway of [an] apartment house. . . . The crowd at this time was screaming and throwing bottles hysterically at the officers.

The young man in this second incident ended up being charged with three counts of battery on a police officer and with resisting arrest, disturbing the peace, and profanity. According to the narrative, the occasion for the man's arrest was his loud use of salty language and his location in the middle of the street. What the narrative neglected to mention was that the encounter with the young man had been initiated by another officer, who had waded into the crowd and singled out the man, provoking him into becoming a "ringleader," who volubly objected to the unsolicited

---

[2] The inclusion of expletives in arrest reports is not only designed to enhance verisimilitude of narratives but also helps to concretize charges of profanity as a rationale for arresting the defendant.

police presence. This situation created a preemptive precondition and precedent for the officer who next arrived on the scene:

> All I saw was a standoff between the policeman who'd been on a week and this other juvenile. Now, you can't let the juvenile go—here it was after 10 o'clock; I think it was after curfew. He's already riled up the rest of the group there; he's an instigator. Now, if you take the leader away, you don't have the group. So we had to get rid of him.

The attempts to corral the young man who had been intercepted by the first officer resulted in an utterly confusing and demeaning chase, which in turn invited a supportive and indignant choral accompaniment:

> So I got him around this way to try to get him, and meanwhile he's yelling everything in the book that you could think of. And this is exciting the crowd. I guess they like to see the police fight their hero here. . . . And I don't know what it was, he started running. He started running down the street, and he started screaming for his mother: "Mommy, Mommy, Mommy!"

The pursuit ended in the apartment-house lobby where the young man had unsuccessfully tried to take refuge:

> There's nowhere for him to go. So we get him handcuffed and he's still screaming and yelling. So we bring him outside, and bricks and everything else were flying. So guess who's the only one who got hit? He is, lucky for us. He got hit, and we got him back to the car and he's still wild as anything. So we had the wagon come. The wagon came, [we] put him in the wagon, and brought him down to jail.
>
> Well, I saw him about a half hour later. A completely different person—humble, mild, subdued, just complacent, and that is about it. He just changed completely.

The de-escalation in the young man's response to his predicament (and his plaintive appeal to his mother) raised questions in the officer's mind about his initial assessment of the man as a rational person and a leader of men and about his capacity for premeditated incitement. However, it also became obvious that gaining a sympathetic response from spectators did not require rationality or intent. Anyone who might be credibly perceived as having been arbitrarily singled out for police attention would be entitled to the support of his peers, including the tangible support of the brick-throwing members of the group. As the officer put it in his interview,

P5:[3] They were excitable. If—let's say—we had hit him, we would have had an incident on our hands.

Interviewer: You say they were throwing rocks?

P5: Throwing rocks, anything they could get they were throwing at the officer. They couldn't care. It could have been me, you, anybody else. If you'd had the uniform, you'd have been thrown at.

Interviewer: What were you thinking about at this time?

P5: Wish I had my car closer.

Interviewer: You were thinking about getting him into the car.

P5: Into the car and out of there. I'd lost my hat. I lost my hat that night. Had to go out and buy a new hat.

The incident served to exemplify the thin line that could separate a group of angry spectators from angry initiators of a riot. According to the officer, "The crowd was exciting me because I know this crowd. I've dealt with them enough in the last 3 weeks and each time they're getting bolder and bolder. I mean, they're getting nasty." By way of documentation, the officer described a more recent experience in which he and another officer encountered an intoxicated gang member who had been sleeping in the back of a car that they had stopped in the vicinity of the gang's club house. When the officers attempted to arrest the man, the encounter drew the hostile attention of his colleagues:

> Anyway, all these kids need is something like this. And they started to come over and jump around and yell and scream. And you ought to hear the things they say. They want to blow up our car. They don't think nothing of killing policemen or any other thing. But they need

---

[3] Numbers indicate different officers who were numbered sequentially in the original study.

someone to lead them. They won't do this if they're not in a crowd. I've got them separated and they're different kids.

The incident culminated when the ostensibly incapacitated arrestee staged a Houdini-like escape from the police car:

So, anyway, I put the kid in the car, and I don't know how he did it—he must be a magician or something—but he put the window down without any handle. He did it. I don't know how he did it, but he did it.

This attempt to evade police custody drew predictably enthusiastic support from the man's friends, and the officers' efforts to prevent the escape elicited predictably wrathful indignation:

Once my partner put his hand down to get him back in the car—you know, he was half out the window, mind you—this did it. They started closing in on us; they started throwing rocks, started throwing rocks at the car and everything else. I told them to get back on the sidewalk. No, they wouldn't go back on the sidewalk. . . . So I get the big night club up like this and I say, "Get back there." Well, they didn't move. . . . Actually, I think if I had hit one of them or somebody else would have hit one of those other kids with a club, I wouldn't be here right now. It would have been bedlam. This was going through my mind too. That was the reason I held back: I didn't want to incite anything. I figured if I didn't have to, I wasn't going to do it.

In a situation such as this, the "basic" scenario in the minds of officers acquires a new addendum, in which the distinction between hostile spectatorship and participation in the confrontation is officially obliterated and members of the chorus are defined as legitimate targets—or potential legitimate targets—of police action.

"THE CHORUS IS UNDER ARREST"

Most police–citizen encounters in the sixties occurred in public places, which meant that the confrontations generally took place in the presence of bystanders. At minimum, the police officers who were involved in these confrontations considered the presence of bystanders to be an inevitable but annoying impediment. However, most officers also felt that spectatorship did not provide anyone with a license to take an immoderate interest in the proceedings. At some level, the average officer assumed that his actions on behalf of law and order ought to be immune from closer inspection, inquiry, or interpolation from members of the public. If and where this norm discouraging pesky spectatorship was violated, transgressors were usually informed that they had been interfering with the officers' work, which meant that they were now morally and legally entitled to be arrested.

The following excerpted report provides a case in point:

> [The officers] were issuing a traffic citation to [an offender] when the suspect came upon the scene with a group of friends. The suspect approached the police vehicle in which [the original offender] was being questioned and wanted to know what the problem was. He was advised that the issue was one of traffic violations and kept asking for details and was told to leave the area near the police vehicle so the issue could be concluded. After being told to leave a second time, he did so reluctantly and muttered under his breath. . . . [Later, he] returned from across the street and again attempted to interfere with the officer to the point of using profanity and refusing to leave the area, and when [the officers] told him to leave he stated, "Fuck all you cops," and drew back his fist in a threatening manner.

According to one of the officers who participated in this incident, it degenerated after the original offender had reluctantly signed a traffic citation and was waiting for the computer to confirm that he had no outstanding warrants:

P11: Some of his buddies who were driving with him come back across the street—four or five of them. And one of them set himself up as spokesman for the group. About four of them just stayed in the back, and the other one says, "What's going on?" We told him, "This a friend of yours?" He said, "Yeah." We said, "We're writing him out a traffic violation; it doesn't involve you." He said, "Yeah, these cops got me. They're trying to put something on me that I didn't do."

Interviewer: This is the guy in the backseat?

P11: In the backseat of the car. He was relating this information to his friend. I told him, "Look, you'll have to leave the area until we complete this. You can talk to him after we are finished." And he said, "Well, I don't know. I want to know what's going on; I want to know about this ticket." I said, "Well, you don't have to know about this ticket. It doesn't concern you. Get back across the street, because you are interfering with our duties." Well, finally I had to get out of the backseat of the car and approach the guy and tell him to stand up and tell him, "Look, you're going to have to leave this area or else you're interfering with our duties, and you're going to have to suffer the consequences."

The person who took it upon himself to "interfere" had twice been put on notice that this transgression was placing him in jeopardy, but he appeared not to take the warnings seriously:

Interviewer: So now the group starts to come back across the street?

P11: Yeah.

Interviewer: And the leader comes forward?

P11: The same one, yeah. . . . He says, "What have you done to him? I want to go help him." I said, "No, the best thing to do is just stay away. Don't involve yourself."

The man's persistence culminated in his arrest after he ignored the final warning and made a move attempting to translate his Samaritan inclinations into action:

> [He] walks around the car and approaches [his friend] and tries to put his hands on him. At this time I walked right up to him and I says, "Get out of here, or you're going to jail." And then he puts up his dukes, "You ain't taking me nowhere." He didn't throw any punches. I just jumped right on him, and another policeman there jumped on him, and he grabbed his arms so I could put the handcuffs on him.

The prevailing practice of arresting spectators who insisted on pestering the officers or were perceived as getting in their way required drawing scholastic distinctions in determining which of several headings to use in effectuating the arrests:

Interviewer: How do you decide which charge to lodge?

P9: Well, resisting arrest is so broad. I mean, you can have somebody that as you're trying to do your job, even at a traffic accident, where he starts interfering, and, "No, you're not supposed to do this," or starts, "No, it was this. What the hell are you doing?" And he starts getting heavy with the officer. This is when you give them a warning for interfering and tell them, "Let's go or you're going to get arrested." Simply give them a warning on a verbal interfering.

On the physical interfering, well, this is self-explanatory. . . . If I had got a hold of him and he starts messing me up by throwing me around or connecting on some of his swings, the resisting arrest wouldn't be charged. I'd charge him with a battery on a police officer. So this is just anybody that really interferes when you're properly doing your duties, and he interferes, obstructs. This is where your definition comes in there.

Given these flexible interpretations of charges, and the pressure to expedite one's encounters so as to reduce the chances for chorus formation, many officers yielded to the temptation to arrest inconvenient bystanders, though their arrests were unlikely to eventuate in prosecutions:

P12: I says, "Okay, you just get away from here or you're going to go to jail too for interfering." So he kept coming up and I'm saying, "I told you, you're going to go to jail for interfering." So the other officer comes back and he kept persisting. So he went to jail for interfering. No trouble with him; he just went to the car and sat down.

COMPETING MUTUAL SUPPORT

Rank-and-file police officers are apt to be appreciatively aware of their dependence on other police officers, who they know stand ready to offer them support and assistance when they need it. As Egon Bittner (1980) pointed out:

Policing is a dangerous occupation and the availability of unquestioned support and loyalty is not something officers could readily do without. In the heat of action it is not possible to arrange, from case to case, for the supply of support, nor can the supply of such support be made dependent on whether the cooperating agents agree about abstract principles. The governing consideration must be that as longs as "one of us" is in peril, right or wrong, he deserves help. (p. 63)

Most police officers tend to feel a strong sense of kinship, a commonality that is both exclusive and inclusive, a kinship that is largely cemented by work experiences that only the officers can share and that unites them by similarities of personal problems. Unsurprisingly, the informal organization that underlies police agencies as formal organizations reliably features a salient culture that heavily values group loyalty and solidarity:

When you arrive there, it's not only just you looking at this man that's beating a policeman, but you get pretty excited inside because this [officer] is working alongside of you, and you probably know the family and been at his house at one time or another, or maybe he's even a guy that you graduated with in your same class. But that's the first thing you think of, that you do to the man: Get him away from the guy.

The cultural emphasis on police officer interdependence was reinforced in the sixties by the manifest hostility of spectators who surrounded the officers in some neighborhoods:

In this city, and I'm sure it's the same everywhere that the men try to stick pretty close together because it appears more and more every day that you're liable to get injured and that you're going to need help. And the feeling of the crowd there: First there's one and then there's two, and pretty soon there's 10 or 20, and you're pretty sure that they're going to try and get your prisoner.

Police departments in the 1960s were embedded in diverse communities that often contained other informal organizations with salient cultures that valued group loyalty and solidarity. In such communities, the intersection between the loyalties of these indigenous groups and those of policing often took problematic turns. This was particularly the case where helping behavior motivated by group solidarity could invite arrests for interference. One such incident happened to unfold in front of the police headquarters building:

> It was a few Job Corps people to the left of the police building—they were sitting right in front of it, and one of them was passed out among the flower pots. And there were three or four others sitting around there. . . . I went over and wanted to see—you know—whether the guy had been hit or knocked out or whether he had drunk too much and passed out. So, some of the other Job Corps people told me to get away from him. And I said, well, I was going to talk to him, and they weren't needed any more, so why didn't they move into one of the other flower boxes. They didn't want to do that. And so I decided I'd take him inside and talk to him in there, get him away from these idiots. And they decided that I wasn't going to take him in. . . . And so I told them that they had better get over there or they were going to get arrested for interfering.

The officer decided to effectuate an arrest for drunkenness despite the repeated requests of members of the group to let them take care of their friend:

> Well, I shake him by the shoulder and say, "Hey, champ, wake up." He mumbles and falls back down again. They say, "Hey, let him go. We'll take care of him." And I said, "No, I'd better take him in and take care of it." And they said, "No, you're not going to." Well, I'm going to.

The officer had felt entitled to persevere and said as much. He then attempted to short circuit any incipient confrontation by entering the building. The result was that the ensuing scuffle produced a broken glass door, an injury to the officer, and an out-of-control situation in the police building lobby:

Interviewer: So you walked out of the door again and chased them out of the building.

P14: Yeah. I don't think that the fact that I told them to get out did much. All it did was stop them from coming in, but they didn't go out, they just stopped. I think that what shocked them more than anything was the quantity of blood that was coming out of me here. I took my glove off—a glove about the size of this one here—and held it up to my head, and the cut was on either side here. It wasn't doing a thing for it. I never saw so much blood.

In the interim, the officer had picked out a second member of the group to be arrested for interference:

P14: I placed the first one under arrest for drunk.

Interviewer: And that was after he couldn't pass the test.

P14: Yeah, right. And I physically put the other one under arrest, although I never said anything. See, all you can do is grab one at a time and go back and get another one and take him.

Interviewer: Have you any idea why they fought like they did?

P14: Well, I think they felt quite a brotherhood. They wanted to come in and get that guy away, get him out of trouble.

An analogous transaction involving an effort to rescue a person who was being arrested for intoxication is reported as follows in an arrest report:

> While [the officers] were placing the drunk under arrest, the suspect came up and stated that the drunk was a friend and he would take him home. [The officers] explained that the drunk was under arrest and would have to go to jail. The suspect was told by [the officer] five times to be quiet and to go on home—that there was nothing he could do for his "friend." The suspect stayed and gave [the officer] and other officers verbal harassment. At this point [the officer] explained Section 148P.C. [interfering] to the suspect and told him to leave or he would be arrested on that charge. The suspect continued to talk and give the officers a bad time but was walking away. The suspect walked up behind [a second officer] and placed his hands on [the officer's] back and attempted to push him out of the way. A pushing contest started

and when [a third officer] went to the aid of [the second officer]—his tie was torn from his uniform. . . . At the jail the guy under arrest for 647 P.C. (drunk) stated that he had just met the suspect tonight in a bar.

A drinking acquaintanceship may not officially qualify as an informal organization, but the bond may suffice in some quarters for purposes of generating solidarity norms. We happened to interview the bystander involved in the incident, and he explained that the arrestee "lives around here, like I do, and we all kind of stick together in this neighborhood."

SNOWBALLING UNFAIRNESS

Police officers are often reluctant to back down after they have taken a public stand—even if the position they have assumed may be ethically and legally indefensible. An example of consequences that can accrue from such ill-advised perseverance is provided by a scenario described as follows by the officer who was responsible for the situation:

> I went after this one boy, and I was taking him back to the car, and he was struggling to get away from me, and there were all kinds of people there, and they were grabbing at me and pulling on my arm to free the boy. I got my shirt torn off. They were just screaming and carrying on. And then some other police units arrived—a couple of motorcycles and the wagon. And I arrested the boys and got them into the car and got the father arrested and put him in the wagon for obstructing me, and some other person—I think it was a woman— one of the women I knew had attacked me.

The officer ended up arresting a group of people for interfering with an arrest that he might not have been entitled to make. He nonetheless went on to blame the arrestees, including the father of two small children he had mistakenly accused of concealing information about a stolen car that was parked in the vicinity of their home:

> As a matter of fact, these boys had nothing to do with this car, but I thought they should be arrested in any case. I was making a lawful

arrest, whether the right circumstances or not. I had something to deal with, and they should have submitted to arrest, and they would have been released right there on the scene when it was ascertained. And that father certainly should not have obstructed me, or these other people doing what they did. So I had them all sent down in the wagon, charging them with resisting arrest or obstructing a police officer.

When the wagon the officer had summoned—containing two young boys, their middle-aged father, and one male and one female member of the chorus—arrived at the loading platform of the jail, it quickly occurred to supervising personnel at the scene that processing this group into the facility might be ill advised. It also occurred to them that in this instance the officer's actions could benefit from review:

Interviewer: The boys went to court?

P15: No.

Interviewer: The adults?

P15: No.

Interviewer: Why?

P15: Because after we got them to jail, the captain of the watch heard something about the call, and the prisoners were brought to his office and he questioned them, and he called me in and there were some questions asked, and then he released these people "pending further investigation." . . . The investigation was turned over to the internal affairs division.

Interviewer: How come?

P15: Well, they explained to me we'd get a much more thorough investigation that way and a greater likelihood of a conviction. It wasn't true.

3

A Concern About Police Brutality or Disproportional Police Response

The level of concern of spectators in police–citizen confrontations tends to keep pace with the level of physical conflict that the spectators observe. This means that the more force police officers use, the more likely it is that they will hear expressions of disgruntlement from persons who witness their predations. In the 1960s, the officers were especially likely to encounter expressions of concern because many citizens had concluded that police officers have a predilection for arresting people for very minor violations (see Chapter 2); consequently, questions were likely to arise about the legitimacy of these police interventions, which in turn would provoke the officers to follow up their opening moves with escalating uses of force.

It did not help at the time that many police officers held a compatible view, which postulated that their deployment of force followed almost inexorably from encounters with the pigheadedness and recalcitrance of citizens:

> The thing is, it's your job to enforce the law, and these people are of such a state of mind that eventually force is going to have to be used. I mean, talking might prolong the time before it happens, but it's not

going to change their attitude. If you're going to do your job, if you're going to enforce the law, you're going to have to use force to take them. No amount of talking is going to get them to go along with you . . . .

Arguing gets nobody anywhere. You have to make your stand, be firm in it, know you are right. But to stand and argue with them does no good. I'm not talking about arguing about something intelligent, I'm talking about where the citizen is just standing there berating the officer and cussing and swearing and causing a disturbance, drawing more people, where if definite action were taken earlier, it might prevent some of the crowd and some of the aftermath when you have more people involved in it.[1]

One of the corollaries of these expectations was that many officers felt that one had to proceed expeditiously from one's initial contact with a suspect to the effectuation of an arrest—even if the accelerated sequence required some physical nudging to motivate an uncooperative perpetrator:

P16:[2] And about this time I saw some kids looking over the fence next door. Some people across the street starting to drift over, and I didn't want any part of that act, you know. The guy was under arrest by this time, and we knew if they came over there, there would be a real problem. So I asked him about three or four times to get in the car, and no, he wasn't going to. He called us names a couple of times, and I said, "You're under arrest." He said, "What for?" you know, and I said, "For use of profanity." And he says, "Well, you aren't going to take me to jail." And I said, "Come on, let's go. Get in the car. You're under arrest." "I ain't going to get in your car. You ain't going to put me in no police car.". . . And these people were coming closer and closer. So we grabbed his arm and said, "Let's go."

Interviewer: How large was this crowd?

P16: There were three or four kids, 12 to 14 age group, just peeking over the fence, and then there were a couple across the street [of] about 19 or 20.

---

[1] Again, the excerpts in this chapter are from incident-centered interviews conducted under the auspices of the police department, with the support and sponsorship of the National Institute of Mental Health Center for the Study of Crime and Delinquency.

[2] Numbers still indicate different officers who were numbered sequentially in the original study.

And then there were people coming out of houses—they were looking up this way . . . the 19- to 20-year-olds started across. I knew exactly where they were headed.

Interviewer: And you felt that they might have got into it?

P16: Oh, this is not written into any departmental policy, but anybody who works neighborhoods like this knows: If you make an arrest and there's going to be conflict, you better get the guy out of there, because if you stay there and argue with them—they come crowding around— you've had it. You've got to—bang!—get the guy out, lay a strip of rubber down the street. I've done that.

Unfortunately, the prescription ("get the guy out") could present logistical problems when the individual at issue steadfastly indicated that he had no desire to leave:

> After telling him about three or four times to get in the car, I reached for his arm, I said, "Come on, let's get in the car." And he pushed his arm up trying to get my arm away, and then I grabbed him again and it was on. He wasn't actually trying to hit me or anything but just resisting. And I held him in a choke hold, and my partner put the cuffs on him, and we picked him up like a load of half of a beef. Loaded him in the back, slammed the doors, jumped in, and the car was gone.

It is ironic that in this scenario the officers' strategy for avoiding the scrutiny of spectators would almost invariably lead to physical confrontations, which would provoke a riot or two if the officers had remained on the scene. But as the officers saw it, if they were unable to leave in time with the arrestee in tow, the arrestee would be responsible for promoting any ensuing riot by playing to the crowd, thus forcing the officers to use additional physical force:

> If you stay there over that limit and most of the time you're there your prisoner is real difficult, you might have a riot. It could create a riot because this guy won't come along with you now. He's not going to draw this large crowd and then meekly go with the police. He's drawing this crowd to show them that he's a man and nobody's going

to get the best of him. So then you're going to have a real go with the guy, and while you're trying to wrestle the guy you might have to use a bit of force. . . . Now they don't even know why you are arresting the guy. He might have just murdered his mother—they don't know. But they come over to see, and they see a guy resisting and a policeman say, "Come on, let's go." And if you use force to shove him along, all of a sudden that's brutality, see. And all of a sudden the mob is completely on his side, and now you've got maybe 20 or 30 people to contend with instead of just one. This is why most of the time— I don't care if the guy was just shooting a BB gun—if he doesn't get in the car, I get him in the car and I get out of there.

MANHANDLING VULNERABLE OPPONENTS

In situations such as the one described, the challenge the officers faced was to dislodge or displace an individual who did not wish to be moved. In the process, they had to deal with the person as if he were an inanimate object. From a bystander's perspective, this spectacle of forceful translocation could appear to involve a violation of a person's dignity, as well as being transparently one sided and unfair. The impression of unfairness would be exacerbated where the subject being moved was badly outnumbered by the police.

P18: The image is bad enough. The image is worse when there's three policemen and one guy fighting, although people may not realize that the older you get you're not as swift as you were. Now, here's a 21-year-old sailor in pink condition, and he's big, and he's tough. And you're dealing with guys in their 30s, and sure, we're a little soft and maybe not just as quick, and so, consequently, we've got our work cut out for us. And even more so where the person involved was female.

P7: [With] a woman you can't use the same type of force that you do on a man. With a man it's fairly simple. If he insists on fighting, the reasonable thing to do is belt him over the head with the club once, and it would have ended all the situation. We can't do this with a woman. We have to put up with her biting and scratching.

P16: After we got her out of the car there were four police—two on the arms and legs—and we carried her over to the wagon. . . . Now the names are coming. They looked at me and [said], "Punk!" You know: "What you beating on that woman for?" I said, "We're not beating on her, we're restraining her, we're holding her." But you can imagine these four policemen with a woman. Everyone thinks of a woman as a mild, meek little thing, no matter how large she is. But I've seen women who had a better right hand than Cassius Clay ever dreamed of. So, she's a big woman and she's strong. We're holding her—you know—we're just trying to hold on to her. And these people are calling us punks.

The impression that officers are devoid of chivalry could become unavoidable where a man–woman encounter degenerated into an angry wrestling match, as in the following situation, which involved an intervening spectator:

P29: I just told her to stay out of it.

Interviewer: Did she say anything to you?

P29: Oh, something to the effect that they can't treat her friends like that, or she's going to help her friends, and there's nothing I can do to stop her, and you know, she's just yelling back and forth. I'm telling her to shut up.

The scenario, as it became available for the inspection of bystanders, could not be plausibly interpreted as an act of self-defense by the police:

P29: Well, I tried grabbing her wrists from the front. This is where she started kicking me, and so I just pushed her to the ground, and she kept kicking. Laying on her back on the ground, she was still kicking up at my groin. I had dirt all over the front of my pants between the knee and the waist where she was kicking me. So I rolled her over on her face and got her arms behind her back and was holding her arms.

Interviewer: Is she saying anything?

P26: Oh, she's cussing, screaming about the m-f police and everything.

Interviewer: Is this drawing a crowd?

P26: Oh, we had about 120 people watching by this time.

A SHARED SENSE OF VICTIMIZATION

The most persuasive brutality scenario is one in which substantial force is being used and the person against whom force is deployed declares himself in immediate need of assistance:

P18: I get right on top of him and he's still fighting, and I hit him about three times. I've got him knocked kind of silly, and I get up in a crouch; I roll him over, I get one arm behind him, I get the cuffs on him, and then I get the other arm up and get the cuffs on that arm. I've got him handcuffed. I look up . . .

Interviewer: Now you notice the crowd.

P18: There are a bunch of unfriendly faces around me, and this is when he starts playing directly to the crowd.

Interviewer: He comes out of his stupor a little bit.

P18: Right, and he's hollering, "Don't let him take me. Look what he's doing to me." And the crowd is noisy too. You know: "Man, you ain't got no right to do that. What you doing that for," and "Look at what that White policeman's doing to that poor man," and this sort of thing. Then as I say, this thing is getting pretty touchy, and I'm scared—definitely scared—and I don't even know if my arm is any good. I'm in a state of semishock too. Well, someone in the crowd says, "Let's get him." That's when I drew my service revolver.

The impression of police brutality conveyed by the unsavory particulars of a physical confrontation can be verbally reinforced by the running commentary of protagonists who have jaundiced preconceptions of the police. Such appears to have been the case with a seemingly inauspicious traffic stop involving a resistant female driver:

She says, "You must be from Alabama—you pick on us Black folks all the time." I said, "Ma'am, may I see your driver's license?" "I'm not showing you nothing." I said, "Ma'am, all I want to see is your driver's license." She said, "What did I do?" I said, "Well, in the first place, you were driving on the wrong side of the street, and in the second place, you cut right in front of me. I had to slam on the brakes to avoid hitting you." "I don't care what the hell I did. What did you stop me for?"

An altercation eventuated from this encounter, and the officer ended up attempting to detain the woman:

P5: I said, "Come back to the car." And that's when I—like they say, when you put your hand on them, this happens. Well, sometimes you have no other choice. I mean, she wasn't going to sign that citation. She was taking off. I asked her and I asked her and I asked her. I didn't want to even touch her.

Interviewer: Then the touching came when she was walking away?

P5: Well, when she was going the other way. She was half way up the block.

Interviewer: And that's when she became wild?

P5: Right. Half way up the block, and here again we were half a block from the car, and when we got back she was yelling all these things: "All you Negroes going to stand around and let these m-f cops push me around?" And she kept yelling and screaming this.

As the officer involved saw the unfolding situation, the woman's allegation of police brutality was wildly inapplicable to himself, given the restraint that he felt he had employed:

> I've never seen anybody treated so easily and so nonviolently and then get so violent in my life. I couldn't believe it. I mean, other than just getting her back to the car, that is all I ever did to her. And yet, she kept getting wilder and wilder as time progressed. And the crowd kept getting bigger.

The officer attributed the self-control that he thought he had been exercising to his awareness of special sensitivities of spectators in the neighborhood, which he hypothesized had to do a with mother fixation and the shape of African-American family constellations:

> You don't dare do anything to a woman that's in her 50s, in an all-Negro area. Because you know how they like their mamas—the

matriarchal society they have there. So I'm looking around and I see the people start moving in, so I just say, "Well, I'll just walk her back; she can't hurt me that much," because I was being careful. . . . And so it took four of us to handcuff her cause she just kept squirming, and you didn't want to hurt her, and you kept doing this and that, and boy, the crowd was getting hostile. I mean, they were yelling and screaming. I mean, it was getting kind of violent. So, when the wagon got there, we just took off. I said, "Let's get out of here; we don't want to upset these people anymore."

Where police officers—as in this case—terminate a confrontation by precipitously fleeing the scene with an arrestee, their departure is liable to leave in its wake a crowd of spectators with unresolved frustrations and unappeased anger—feelings that tend to color subsequent experiences in which police officers seem more and more like unmitigated bullies. Such reminiscences give rise to accounts that are disseminated, and cumulatively contribute to the unfavorable reputation of police departments.

CO-OPTING THE CHORUS

Most spectators in the sixties who engaged in running comments about ongoing confrontations were apt to be critical of the police, especially when witnessing police officers deploying physical force. However, such was not inevitably the case: Some bystanders were able to reserve judgment or give the police the benefit of doubt. There were even instances in which individual spectators intervened on the officers' behalf, especially when they had witnessed the provocation to which the officers responded:

P7: If the crowd is there before we arrive and can see just what goes on, then there's no problem whether it's an all-Colored neighborhood or White [provided] they see what the cause of the whole problem is. In fact, I have had incidents in some of these bars down there—they're probably the worst in the city—where we've gone in there and some guy picks a beef with us for no apparent reason, and the crowd sits down saying, "That man started it—he's wrong." If they see the whole thing, there is very seldom a problem with the crowd. But if the crowd gathers and only sees the latter part of it where the police are winning the beef, they draw the immediate conclusion of police brutality.

P13: In this particular instance the lady . . . went up to these guys that were mouthing off (she's Colored,) and she says, "Why you damn fools," she says, "He [the officer] was protecting me." She says, "That man was going to beat up on me." And she says, "He's only doing his job." And you know something, this took all the wind out of his sails, and it took the wind out of all of them. . . . This stopped the whole thing. These guys didn't have anything more to say.

P25: And they started, you know, calling us all kinds of names and giving us a bad time. The only thing that saved us from having a big fight right there with them was that two other Colored fellows—but older men— were across the street and saw the whole thing, and they came over in our defense. And otherwise we'd have had trouble there. But they came over and they told these kids that they were all wrong and that they had no business talking that way and acting that way—and that settled that. Otherwise, that could have been a real bad one.

Officers reported one or two occasions on which some members of the chorus had adjudged the police the lesser of two evils or some spectators had deemed them to have exercised commendable restraint or to be more deserving of sympathy or compassion than the perpetrator who was being arrested. However, in such instances, the support for law and order typically tended to be discretely and privately communicated to the officers:

P4: And at this point I heard one Negro man, probably about in the middle 20s, who came forward from the crowd and peered in back of the wagon and said, "Officer, why didn't you shoot that man? I saw the knife he had. I know he always carries a knife. . . . Man, I wouldn't have fought him. I would have killed him." And another one says, "Man, why didn't you club him? You should have hit that man. This man is as strong as a bull." And approximately four teenage girls approached . . . and offered to give us any information we needed because, well, I had my hand crushed, and one of the other officers had his uniform torn. . . . One of them was concerned that I was injured. . . . But they wanted to offer their assistance because they observed it and thought that it was done without unnecessary injury to the man.

Where officers had intervened in situations in response to complaints from a citizen, they could generally count on some measure of support— at least from the person or persons who had requested their assistance. However, friendly choral support was not necessarily assured over the long run, especially when encounters later degenerated into free-for-alls in which the prospective arrestee ended up being injured. Continued support for the officers was even less assured when supportive citizens found themselves having to compete with an unexpected groundswell of anti-police sentiment, as in the following incident of domestic violence:

P3: When I got out of the car I could hear this loud screaming. There was yelling and shouting, and I heard something break.

Interviewer: Did this situation look explosive to you, with these people milling about?

P3: Definitely. . . . This was at least a potential Watts-type incident.

In this case, the officers took note that the tide had turned against them. Their concern deepened after they had forcibly subdued their man and pondered the prospects of carrying him through a visibly hostile crowd:

> And the next thing that occurred in my mind was to get him out of the house and into the car and eventually into the paddy wagon and get him the heck out of there, because this crowd outside had already begun hooting and hollering, and I had visions of my police car being overturned. . . . And there were some comments being made out in the street—something derogatory towards the police department.

It was at this stage that one of the officers decided that it might be a good idea to enlist some promising candidates for an actively supportive chorus:

> And so I thought, well, this wouldn't look too good for us to be carrying this individual down the stairs because the crowd outside—as is usually the case, not knowing what's going on—they'll side against

the police department, and we were liable to have an incident here that's liable to get nasty. And so I told the father and this other man, whoever he was . . . to carry [the suspect] down the stairs. This way we would look clean and pure. The individual was being carried down the stairs—and a couple of policemen with their arms folded. And we looked like sweet little innocent babes.

As this gambit unfolded, the officers and the arrestee found themselves engaged in competing efforts to attract the sympathy and to gain the support of spectators:

P3: And the whole while they were carrying him down the stairs, he was writhing about. He was yelling, screaming at the top of his voice, obviously trying to agitate the crowd and in some parts succeeding. He was yelling, "Look, Black people, what these White m-fs are doing to me."

Interviewer: While these two other Black people were carrying him out?

P3: Yeah. He said, "Look what these White m-fs are doing to me! They are beating me up! Look what they are doing to me! Help me, help me!"

Once the arrestee had been placed in the police car, he intensified his appeals while making futile but demonstrative efforts to escape. In the process, the man garnered growing support, especially from younger members of the crowd:

And the windows shook and the foundations and whole car was shaking, and he's still swearing . . . "We're going to have another Watts right here. I'm going to start it." And he's going on like this. And he succeeded in getting this crowd worked up. There's a lot of hooting and hollering going on by this 18-, 19-, 20-year age group right around the periphery of the crowd.

After the man was transferred to the wagon and the wagon was driven out of range, he continued to target his appeals to members of an increasingly younger generation:

So while we're there, some little kids come along on their bicycles— little boys, little girls, half a dozen of them maybe, 10, 12 years old—

and this guy is looking out the window, and I guess he sees these kids and he says, "Help me, help me, get somebody to help me." He starts swearing: He says, "Look what these m-f cops are doing to me." He says this to the kids. The kids weren't old enough to understand what was going on, but I guess they got scared and took off.

The arrest report relating to this volatile incident carried the following notation: "While awaiting the arrival of wagon, unidentified [Black males] in their 20s made a move as if to aid the prisoner. They disappeared as [a motorcycle] officer rode up. [The] situation had riot potential." A more telling note could have been appended to the report crediting the officers with initiative for recruiting allies among the spectators. This intervention deserved special mention, not only because it unquestionably affected the outcome of the encounter but also because it presaged what subsequently became salient developments in the field, involving varied efforts by the police to reach out to the community.

4

Sensing an Unbridgeable Divide

Cross-sectional views of historical events can be misleading if one overlooks the fact that the past has a past of its own—at least as the past is experienced by its protagonists. In the sixties, police officers and the members of the community who observed them and who resented and resisted their interventions experienced their own situations and saw each other partly as the culmination of trends, of cumulating developments that they generally felt were unwelcome but inexorable.

THE IMPOTENCE OF OMNIPOTENCE

It is a surprising paradox that police officers of the period—the officers whose heavy-handed interventions may strike us in retrospect as cavalier and out of control—could describe themselves consistently as cornered and beleaguered. The proverbial chorus (whose members were occasionally arrested for interfering) was perceived by the officers as being ominous and threatening, not only because the hostility of spectators carried riot potential but also because the attitudes they expressed suggested that groups in the community were prepared to question the authority of the police. This challenge to police authority by citizens in turn appeared congruent with trends in the criminal justice system that threatened to handicap the police:

P8:[1] And civil rights and rights in general are more and more being brought to the front, or it seems to have been more emphasized lately. Now, the policeman is sort of caught in the middle, because while he is trying to do a job for most citizens, he's taking the rights away from those few that he comes in contact with. And the way it seems to be, as far as executing the law, [is] to hold off more and more in favor of the defendant. And I don't want to say, make things easier for them, but make for less chance of mistake, let's say. . . . [This] makes it almost impossible for someone to be wrongly accused and wrongly sentenced. But at the same time, that puts us on edge and pulls us off balance. The policeman may be right or wrong—I don't know. As far as trying to do the job, it makes it harder. But by the same token, it lets everybody that you come in contact with think they have more of an edge over this policeman.

P24: They hear that their civil rights are being violated and this type of thing. That may be true, but it's also true that we have a job to do. . . . Hard feelings are going to continue to develop between the public and the police in some instances because nobody likes to see his brother, his mother, his uncle, or his aunt is going to have to be taken to jail. This always put the policeman in the part of the villain. Now, I think the only way we can overcome this is to educate the people, to make them realize there is, in my opinion, a moral decay in our society, in some segments of our society. I think we have to overcome that. I don't know how.

P3: This type of police agitation and this cliché that goes around about police brutality and all this agitation that goes on, the civil rights movement and some of these communist-inspired operations not only here but [also] over the country—I feel that these things can explode most any kind of police incident where a police is arresting [a] Negro—if a White policeman, I should say, is arresting a Negro.

---

[1] Numbers again indicate different officers who were numbered sequentially in the original study.

P31: If you were just walking down the street and you were assaulted, you'd naturally think—and most people would—to fight back. If I am arresting somebody and I'm assaulted and I hit back, right away that is no longer self-defense, this [is] police brutality. . . . "Police brutality" is a mass hysteria.

P13: I guess, you know, they want a police review board here, and they got some of these guys agitating in the area, and he says, "This is why we need a police review board, that's why we need a police review board."[2]

In the course of accounts in which officers described themselves as physically overpowering and carting off miscreants and persons who had tried to interfere with their activities, they concurrently portrayed themselves as escaping in the nick of time—mostly by summoning sizeable reinforcements. In these narratives, the average encounter with officers in the community sounds extremely hazardous and—in the long run—hopeless. As one officer put it, "Get a little crowd around and you can push the cops clear out of town." The future of policing in these narratives begins to sound like the story of an army that has been forced into retreat (the Greek chorus would say a *katabasis*), and each incident in which spectators are involved is presented as the police equivalent of Custer's Last Stand—a key difference being that Custer thought that he might eventually prevail, whereas the officers felt that they were outgunned and disadvantaged:

P26: You just can't tell them anymore because they say, "Well, go pound salt.". . . A policeman being there means absolutely nothing. I mean, they have no more respect for a police officer than [for] the man in the moon. . . . You're kind of dangling when you're handling a Negro. And the first thing that comes to mind [is]: "I know that he's going to come out on top"—you know, in a way. I don't know why, but you have that feeling. And so you always try to back off a little more rather than be aggressive.

---

[2] These and other excerpts in this chapter again derive from incident-centered interviews conducted under the auspices of the police department, with the support and sponsorship from the National Institute of Mental Health (NIMH) Center for the Study of Crime and Delinquency.

P31: They're becoming more uncooperative, more—how would you say—antagonistic, showing more hate for you than I've ever known. Just in this past year, just in talking to some average kids, like stopping a kid on the street, ask[ing] him for his ID. . . . Sometimes, you know, they come off the wall with this, "You can't talk to me," and all this stuff. And you know, you begin to wonder why. It just seems to be growing.

Interviewer: Why do you think it is?

P31: Why? Sign of the times, I guess.

"Sign of the times" was not an entirely satisfactory précis of the experience the officers were trying to summarize. The officers advanced a number of hypotheses to account for the growing antagonism they felt they were experiencing. Quite predictably, none of the hypotheses made room for the possibility that police practices might be playing some role in making people angry. Favored explanations tended to be sociological or psychological analyses and tended to focus on citizens, prominently including the proposition that the youngest members of the community were being socialized from the cradle to be police haters and were being brought up to disrespect and challenge the police.

P22: That starts way back with their environment, their upbringing. A few years back, I think, when it first started, children were brought up with the idea that police are bad, the police are your enemies. Hate the police. And I think these particular individuals have grown up and they are in the, say, 15-to-24 age bracket. There's where you have your trouble: your late teens and your early 20s. . . . The young ones nowadays are listening to their big brothers, and they are beginning to hate.

P12: They're taught to disrespect law and order and policemen from the time they are old enough to understand anything. Fourth of July, over at the park, we are walking riot patrol. Another rookie and myself were walking along. Just some little baby, maybe 2 years old or maybe a little older, as we come walking by: "M-f cop" . . . It all comes from the way they are taught. And how you are going to undo this overnight? I don't know.

P7: Where the White policeman is always suppressing the poor under-privileged Black man and so on. I think this is drummed in their heads from their childhood. And they do need a scapegoat, and I think that's where they pick on the policeman.

The proposition that the police serve as designated scapegoats is conso-nant with the premise that antipolice sentiment has nothing to do with actions of the police but has everything to do with prejudments shared among minority citizens. The officers could not circumvent the phenome-non of chorus formation, nor evade the observation that spectators to their encounters tended to arrive at a disquieting consensus about the unfairness of officers and the reprehensibility of their behavior. In speculating about this solidarity among spectators, a few of the officers resorted to ethnic stereo-types relating to in-group loyalties and restlessness and a need for excitement:

P4: The Negro has a way of getting one another to do things without ever having met the person before. 'Cause I've had situations where I've had prisoners, having people trying to get doors open on patrol cars. And after the situation has all calmed down, the person is from out of state, from out of the city, and has never seen the suspect before. I've never had a situation involving a Mexican, or Whites, Orientals, or any other race where a person can gain control of another's confidence enough to get him to react enough to assist you in fighting a police officer or in trying to escape or trying to destroy evidence or anything else. . . . I've had situations where I took one of eight Cherokee Indians into custody, and they [had] just been involved in a large fight, and there was no call at all to assist him. As a matter of fact, one told him, "All right, you got yourself into it, big mouth, now you just get yourself out of it."

P21: It's the young crowd, it's the Negroes. They're out there on the street, they're looking for something to do, they're looking for trouble. This is their way of life. . . . You have a fuse box right there. You have five or six young guys looking for something to do and a policeman comes along and talks to one, regardless of who it is; if he gets involved with them, you've lit the fuse, now you've got the dynamite. Then all it takes is just a little spark and, bingo, there you go . . . and you can't take the time out to explain to them. You can't do it. If I explained to everybody what I was doing and why I was doing it, I wouldn't get anything done, you know. And I don't know what the solution is, I really don't.

A more sophisticated narrative emerged when officers took account of the fact that appeals aimed at spectators appeared to resonate or not to resonate with groups that shared different backgrounds and experiences. Once the person who was the object of police attention—or a surrogate acting on the person's behalf—directed a request for support and assistance to bystanders, the success of his or her campaign appeared to hinge on the extent to which spectators found plausibility in the appeal, which in turn seemed to vary with the age and/or ethnicity of the spectators and with attributes of the setting and the neighborhood. Some groups of bystanders appeared to be largely refractory to chorus mobilization:

P4: I would say this was probably the most cooperative crowd I've ever seen. I don't know how really cooperative they were, although we did take statements from witnesses who seemed to be in a more mature middle-20 age group. Most of them worked. Some of them were married; they had children and they lived in a fairly nice neighborhood that they could afford. Not the neighborhood I live in, but they were—some of them—very cooperative.

P21: Well, he's yelling, he's talking loud, and we're right across the street from a donut shop. Now, the donut shop is mostly older people, railroad men; and mostly White people hang out there and older working-class people, so he wasn't having too much success drawing a crowd, but he was trying.

However, some groups were said to contain individuals who were activists, who incited and whipped up other members of the crowd. A few officers even contended that they had been stalked and that attempts had been made to set them up and bait them to record for public dissemination their predictably intemperate responses:

P13: So these guys, any time there's anything in the area (I know because I've had these guys taking movies[3] and I've been baited before on this)

---

[3] The scenario alluded to here is an alleged effort to entrap an officer into taking incriminating actions that could be recorded on film. This scenario is different from those (discussed later) involving the filming of ongoing police–citizen interactions by spectators.

these guys were trying to take movies of me. . . . I'd never seen this guy before and he'd called me by name. And he says, "I'm tired of you down here arresting us all the time." He says, "You're fucking over us all the time." He says, "I can whip your ass right here and now." And I had to look, and I thought, "What the hell is going on here?" You know, there's something phony about this. . . . Up there on top of this window I see these guys in there, these two Colored guys with a camera. And they've got a movie camera.

P17: I says, "What is the matter with you people?" And right away he goes into a big dissertation about racial tension: "The only reason you stopped me is because I'm a Negro and you're White. . . ." And [he] never swore, never swore, never called me no names or nothing. He got off on this racial binge. He had a chip about three miles high. I said, "See you later, champ." I turned around and got in my car and drove off.

THE POLICE SIDE OF THE EQUATION

The officers we interviewed had been nominated because each had an extensive record of confrontations with citizens. In a number of instances, the degenerating encounters in which the officers had been involved had culminated in citizen complaints and administrative reviews. Some of the officers felt that this process provided one more indication of the increasingly inhospitable environment of policing:

> [Citizens] come down here and make a complaint against an officer,
> and right away they get you upstairs, cutting the record, as they say.
> And another thing: They seem to listen more to the complainant or
> the person who's making the report than to you. And you know, you
> are tired of that; you feel, "What the hell's the use?"

The inhospitable environment was envisaged as including judges, who were not always ready to accept the police officers' accounts of confrontations that ended in violence:

> I can't speak of any place other than here, but I feel a lot of times that
> when I get into court, I more than have to justify my actions. I have

to prove to the court that not only what I did was justified but that it was absolutely the only way out. And as you and I both well know, these situations are a little bit hard to prove sometimes. I mean, it's a matter of you've got to play it by ear on the street, and then when you get into court, you've had 3 or 4 months to think about it, you've gotten tired of legal minds advising you; certainly there might have been another way to handle it. But at that time, on the street, you handle it exactly the way you would if it came up again, 'cause you don't have the time, you don't have the capabilities to sit back for 3 months and analyze every possible situation and take these and quarterback the thing. You have to take it as you see it. And a lot of times the judges take the attitude that the policeman is the aggressor rather than the defendant. I've been to court many times where I've felt that the court was aggressive toward me because I picked on this fellow. . . . They pay me to enforce the law, I go out and I do this, and I lock the guy up, and maybe there's no question of anything physical—maybe it's just a violation or something—and the court feels that, "What the hell did you bother this guy for?" And it's kind of discouraging, you know.

Several officers nonetheless indicated that over the course of their careers they had revised their approaches in day-to-day encounters with citizens. They cited unsatisfactory outcomes of situations in which they had been involved as experiences that they felt had led them to moderate their behavior:

P13: I weigh 210 or [2]15 pounds, and I'd lifted weights and I did a lot of boxing, and I felt I could whip anybody. But it don't work because you can't get out on that street every night and fight. Sooner or later you're going to get hurt, you're going to hurt somebody real bad, or the man upstairs is going to get you up there and he's going to burn you real good. And this is what happened to me. So as I say, as I got older and looked back at my past, I know where the mistakes were. I come on hard. If the guy even looked at me cross-eyed, I thought, "Who the fuck does he think he is?" And right away, I want to chew him up.

P23: When I came on the department, I came on awful strong, and I ran into a lot of trouble. Then I figured something's wrong—it must be me. So then I came out weak, and I found myself in more trouble. So I had to try different things—trial and error. And now . . . the fewer words I say, the better it is. Just let them tell their story, what's on their mind . . . if you listen to them, then they feel you've got their case at heart.

The officers as a rule were not disposed to question the prevailing norms of the police force, but they had no difficulty identifying fellow officers whose modus operandi they considered counterproductive and certain to result in gratuitous conflict and needless violence:

P2: Well, I think some officers come on too strong. I've seen it happen before where some officers don't wait and try to get a hold of the situation. They just come in and grab and say, "You're coming with me," and just grab the person and a lot of times just pop them into the car. But I think some officers do create more of a problem where they have more trouble. Lots of times it's the same officers.

P18: That's what we call around here a "raise-up man." These are the kind of guys that, no matter what they do, they raise somebody up. I know some officers—you will probably have occasion to interview a few of them, and I'm sure will see for yourself—it's the kind of man that can walk into a room and have everybody dislike him before he opens his mouth.

P27: There are some officers who offend practically everybody they talk to.

Interviewer: What do they do?

P27: Well, one particular officer I'm thinking of had numerous resisting arrests. He's had numerous people refuse to sign citations whereupon they had to be taken to jail or had the sergeant come at least and try and talk them into it.

Interviewer: What does he do?

P27: He's just overbearing.

When the officers were asked to describe the type of individual most apt to engage in problematic behavior, the largely older officers tended to nominate largely younger officers, whose instincts they felt had not been seasoned by wisdom-conferring experiences and who might be over-impressed by their newly minted authority. They also expressed concern about the susceptibility of younger officers to the influence of colleagues who might be setting unfortunate examples:

> Because this guy walks down the street and clobbers everybody, this new man will do the same thing. He gets in this rut and he can't get out; he follows that pattern. People are creatures of habit, and when you teach a kid something, that's the way he is going to do it. You're not going to change it, because it's still there.

Another hypothesis—which may have been most warmly endorsed by the brawniest hulks among our respondents—was that small physical stature was likely to promote the need to overcompensate:

P24: You take an officer who maybe is not physically as big as a brother officer, and this guy might get in a little bit more trouble. First of all, because of his size, he tries to make up for his size in being a little more aggressive and a little heavier, in trying to get across that he can do his job as well as the next guy.

P3: I can think of two people right off hand that are both small, but I would hesitate to say that all small men are cocky.

The presumption that once work habits are formed they could be difficult to change permeated the officers' view of their less-than-admirable colleagues. There was also agreement on the need for the utmost tact and discretion in dealing with the behavior of one's peers to preserve a united front when working with other officers in public settings. The feeling was that when a fellow officer engaged in problematic behavior in the presence of civilians, one would be obliged to let events run their course and to provide any support that might be required, though one might follow up with a delicately worded critique or review session after the fact:

P27: Well, usually, you back your partner 100%. If he decides that he's going to wrestle with somebody you have to back him 100% and get right in there with him. After it's over, that's when you do something about it. You say, "Listen, I don't want to tell you how to do your job, and I don't want you to tell me how to do mine, but boy, you're going to get yourself into a lot of grease, you're going to get me in a lot of grease."

P18: I think if you do it the right way: sit down and have a cup of coffee and just talk about it and explain—you know—there is no personal animosity. I mean: "I would just not like to see you get in trouble, because if you get in trouble, I'm going to get in trouble because I'm going to have to back you, right or wrong." I've backed a lot of wrong moves, but I backed them because it was a police officer; it's that simple.

P19: I'd talk to him. Get him off to one side and straighten him out. Say, "Look, pal, either knock this stuff off or forget it, because I can't ride your beefs. I'm not creating them; you are creating them, so you knock it off". . . . If you make him mad at you, what the hell, but you see, you're trying to help the guy out.

P2: I can think of one situation where [there was] this one officer we had this type of trouble with, but four or five other officers were just sitting around together having coffee one night after work and [his problem] was brought up—and I think it made a difference. I don't think he really realized what he was doing, because other officers would have control of the situation and he would drive up, and it would start all over again. And I don't think he realized what he had been doing, is what it was.

P1: [An officer I was riding with] stopped this car because the fellow didn't have a current license tag on the license plate. He did, however, have the necessary papers, which did indicate that he had gone down and procured these, but they hadn't been sent to him yet. So this answered the entire question. It was ridiculous to keep interrogating the man. . . . And I simply told him that this man had in fact complied with the law, and we can tell him good night. . . . I mean, [my calling this to his attention] was all done in a gentlemanly way, of course. There were no hard feelings about it and there shouldn't have been.

As a general guideline for some of his less-experienced colleagues, a sadder but wiser elder statesman in our sample offered the following all-purpose recommendation:

> Don't go pushing a man around every time you see somebody make an infraction of the law. There's a law there, and if you've got a problem, use that law—that's what it's there for. If you don't have a problem, do the best you can, and let it go. A man doesn't have to go to jail.

5

Rank-and-File Resistance to Community-Relations Reforms

S ix years after we conducted our interviews in the West Coast City police
department,[1] a prominent news magazine published a retrospective
account of events that had taken place in the intervening period. The story
read in part as follows:

> For more years than most of its citizens remember, the police
> department . . . had a well-earned reputation for being one of the
> toughest, roughest, and generally unloved of any city in the nation.
> Storm troopers, they were called by many, and very much like storm
> troopers they behaved. . . . Then three years ago something started
> happening. The result is that the . . . police department now has
> acquired a reputation as a near paragon of police virtue; it has become
> downright zealous in guarding the constitutional rights of suspects
> and repairing the battered relations with the city's large population

---

[1] The name of the "West Coast City" has been changed to protect the anonymity of the participating police
department and its officers. The details of the no-confidence vote (the results, minutes of the meeting,
comments on the ballots), the recruit training program, and the recruit training program review document
must all necessarily remain unattributed as well.

of blacks . . . policemen now find themselves being praised by the very
people who so roundly condemned them in the past. . . . Needless to say,
with things changing so rapidly, it wasn't long before angry rumblings
began within the lower ranks. ("The Gain Mutiny," 1971, p. 35)

On November 5, 1971, the "rumblings" culminated in a membership
meeting of the Police Officers Association. According to the minutes of
the meeting,

> a motion was made and seconded from the floor that a secret ballot be
> prepared for distribution calling for a VOTE OF NO CONFIDENCE
> [in the police chief], [demanding] that he retire immediately upon
> reaching the earliest retirement date; also that the results of the ballot
> be made public.

In compliance with this carefully orchestrated motion, the press was
subsequently informed—after the voting had taken place—that of
719 recorded members of the association, 375 had indicated that they had
no confidence in the chief and that he should resign, against 110 who
admitted that they might still have some confidence in his leadership. The
chief did, however, receive the unanimous endorsement of the 48-member
Black Officers Association, who asserted that efforts to remove the chief
were without cause or merit.

The attempts to force the West Coast City police chief out of office
were unquestionably without merit, but they were not—by any stretch of the
imagination—without cause. The chief had embarked on a single-minded
campaign to enforce wholesale changes in his department in the face of
predictable and cumulating resistance. He had done this relying on the
authority of his office, which—given the paramilitary structure of police
organizations—was considerable. He thus had no real problem securing
and ensuring compliance, but he did not enjoy equivalent success in having
his subordinates internalize his goals.[2]

---

[2] In a groundbreaking article, the psychologist Herbert C. Kelman (1958) distinguished between change
through compliance, change through identification, and change through internalization. The long-term
effectiveness of change through compliance rests on continued monitoring.

What the chief had done was to go further than most enlightened police executives in the country to implement the community-relations model of policing, as it had been outlined in several authoritative documents in the sixties. For example, he emphasized service as an overall goal, to the extent of inscribing the words "Police Service" on his newly repainted (baby blue) police cars. The chief's emphasis was in line with the suggestion of the 1967 Task Force on the Police, President's Commission on Law Enforcement and Administration of Justice, which pointed out the following:

> Many people think of the police first when they are in any kind of trouble; as a result, police departments frequently must relay complaints and refer persons to other government agencies. . . . This kind of public service *should be expanded* so that police who observe conditions on patrol that require attention from other public agencies— uncollected garbage, locked playgrounds, housing code violations, consumer frauds—would take the initiative in reporting them to the appropriate agency. (p. 162, emphasis added)

The President's Commission argued:

> In fact, police officers now spend much of their time in "social work" roles. . . . But an expanded police role must be judged not only by whether it alleviates social conditions but also whether it assists the police community relations. . . . The effect would be to improve police–community relations by reducing the adversary role of the police and by making them part of a broader process than merely arrest and conviction. Consequently, increased experiment with new helping roles for the policeman, especially with youths and ex-offenders, is promising. (Task Force on the Police, President's Commission on Law Enforcement and Administration of Justice, 1967, pp. 162–163)

The degree to which this set of objectives failed to inspire the support of West Coast City officers is reflected in the vitriolic comments many of them appended to their 1971 no-confidence ballots.

CRIME SUPPRESSION VERSUS "SOCIAL WORK": A ZERO-SUM GAME?

The comments regarding departmental orientation showed that many of the respondents thought that delivering "service" and "fighting crime" were mutually exclusive and antithetical goals for any self-respecting police department. On a personal level, the officers angrily made it clear that being invited to perform tasks they felt they could define as "social work" or "sociology" was a deliberate assault on their prized identity as crime fighters and law enforcers, to the benefit of offenders who would profit from the policy. Among the sentiments expressed on the ballots that made this point were the following:[3]

> I don't go along with his policies of coddling the public—the only way the criminal element can be controlled is by force. . . . If I had wanted to work in social work, I'd have grown long hair, not taken a bath, and be like one of the people so I could communicate.

> The liberal crime prevention policies of this chief are not what the citizens want. [If this man does not leave,] taxpayers and businessmen will continue to leave the city in droves or carry guns for their own protection.

> The wasting of manpower in positions that were created to enhance a progressive image rather than solve a pressing crime problem (i.e., violence prevention unit, landlord tenant unit, and consumer fraud detail).

> In general, [they are] policies and decisions . . . to build some kind of super sterile social service agency . . . that will keep criminals laughing for some time to come.

> He has forgotten the two most important factors of a police department: protecting life and property. Instead, he is appeasing the criminal and screwing the police and citizens.

---

[3] Each ballot provided a generous space with the instruction, "Please comment below on your reasons for voting as you have so that the association directors can validly convey your feelings. (Please be as specific as possible.)" All the quoted comments were directly transcribed from the ballots and have not been previously published.

I feel that if the chief is allowed to continue in office, his ultraliberal thinking and policies toward law enforcement and crime prevention will soon result in an unprecedented increase in crime. Certainly, no man is fit to be a chief of police who publicly states . . . that he intends to change the direction of his department from that of fighting crime to that of rendering "services" to the public.

The greatest service we can do for citizens is to reduce the ridiculously high crime rate, and I don't think that a service agency can do that.

It's time for tough law enforcement, not social working. We can make more friends by eliminating crime than serving the social needs of a minority of the minorities.

A tabulation of votes by officials of the union listed "failure to adopt law enforcement role" as a charge leveled against the chief by 44 members and "social work stance" as the principal deficit cited by 37 members.

POLICE–COMMUNITY RELATIONS TRAINING

A key requisite for a community-relations oriented police department as envisaged by the Task Force of the President's Commission on Law Enforcement and the Administration of Justice (1967) was "training that equips the police officers to understand the various kinds of individuals with whom they will come in contact, and the various neighborhoods of the city" (p. 175). The task force argued that "clearly, in the majority of police departments, the amount of time given specifically to human and community relations training must be dramatically increased" (p. 175). The task force wrote:

Before an officer can become expert in deriving the truth from con-flicting statements, in knowing how to handle quarreling spouses and delinquent youths, in determining when an arrest for drunkenness or loitering is useful or necessary and when it will merely harm an individual or inflame a minority community, and in calming tense and hostile crowds, he must acquire information and understanding concerning human relations. It is doubtful that this can be acquired in less than 60 hours. (p. 175)

Recruit training reform had ranked high on the West Coast City chief's agenda, and he had invested a great deal of his time and effort (and resources garnered from the state's council on criminal justice) in an unprecedentedly ambitious revision of his police academy curriculum. The state organization charged with peace officer's standards and training had mandated that 20 hours of recruit training time be dedicated to the topic of community–police relations. The West Coast City police department had on its own provided for a generous segment of 54 hours, which under the auspices of the chief was increased to a total of 159 hours within a period of 4 years.

After carefully conducted evaluations, procedural innovations were also introduced to try to make the learning process more interesting and effective. Key courses (including community relations, constitutional law, and firearms training) were enriched with role-playing exercises, videotapes, and replay discussions. According to a progress report submitted by the department's training division, an entire segment of 30 hours was reserved for simulations of critical incidents, and tailor-made field experiences were devised and introduced, such as the following:

> *A Community Field Experience:*[4] The recruit officer will be given an assignment that will place him in different environments. He will be assigned to solicit assistance from agencies such as the Welfare Department, Department of Human Resources, Missions, and Legal Aid. The experience is designed to create a better understanding of the perspective of those who use the services.
>
> *Internship:* An opportunity will be provided each trainee to work for 1 day in a social service agency such as the County Welfare Department or the [West Coast City] Health Clinic. The purpose of this experience is to expose the recruits to other agencies involved in providing service.
>
> *San Quentin Tour:* To provide an on-site exposure to what it's like "on the inside" of a prison.

---

[4] The Training Academy was arguably upstaged in devising experiential learning exercises by the police chief of Covena, California, who had his officers spend the night in the skid row of a neighboring city, where they were duly harassed by the police department.

The enriched training program initially earned favorable reviews, but this later changed:

> Recruits from a later [cohort] were not as positive toward the program. There was a strong feeling that community relations was overemphasized, and [the recruits] tended to feel that the emphasis had made them reluctant to enforce the law. Many in the group went so far as to advocate more military discipline in the training setting.

An unfortunate incident cemented the opposition:

> While on a field visitation with the public defender's office, a recruit inadvertently heard a police officer from another department make prejudiced remarks while waiting to testify. The recruit reported this to the public defender, and he, in turn, used these remarks to destroy the witness's testimony. Word of this incident spread through the department like wildfire, and numerous officers [inquired,] wanting to know if it was the program's intention to turn out finks.[5]

The recruit training program review document from which this descriptive material is drawn concluded by reporting that "although numerous explanations were offered and the training division established an orientation for beat officers, there is still a large contingent of police officers who view the new program as subversive to 'good police work.'" Unsurprisingly, this theory was vigorously propounded by several of the union members who voted to impeach the chief:

> I feel his policies in the training division are outrageous; thank God the majority of the recruit officers are men and can handle the police job and can tell the difference between the 20 weeks of idealistic, clinical training, and the reality of the [West Coast City] jungle.

> Eight weeks of "overtraining" in community relations at the recruit school . . . misleads officers about relations with citizens.

---

[5] There is a germ of truth in this allegation in that most police chiefs would be happy to bring into being a generation of "finks" who would report the transgressions of other officers. Such a development would understandably be at variance with the high priority assigned in the police culture to the norm of peer solidarity. As one of the officers put it in his no-confidence ballot, "This business of turn your partner in: Horseshit!"

Instead of selling his ideas to the department, he has attempted to "brainwash" rookies with his liberal ideas and then turn them loose in the city with older officers who have no idea what has happened.

The new academy (an innovation of the chief) teaches little of the knowledge needed to become a good police officer but instead stresses a permissive social worker oriented type police officer. So instead of attacking crime on the streets, you understand it, and sweep it under the rug.

Recruits [are] being given the impression we are the criminals; they, the watchdogs.

RECRUITMENT AND PROMOTION OF MINORITY OFFICERS

The reshaping of the West Coast City training program arguably had several purposes, one of which was to try to attenuate the department's aggressive peer culture by having enlightened recruits introduce some cultural diversity in the locker room. The topic of "culture" came up explicitly as a subject for instruction in the academy:

> *The Police Culture:* An examination of the police as a distinct culture. [The course segment] explores the causes and complications of this culture, as well as the various subcultures within it. The role dilemma of the Black officer, e.g., in relation to the minority and nonminority communities, and the nonminority officers, is also discussed.

Many recruits ended up succumbing to the blandishments of the mainline police culture, but most of the Black officers who were recruited during this period appeared to resist the temptation. The recruitment of these officers (and some civilian counterparts) had been an urgent priority for community-relations oriented departments. The Task Force on the Police, President's Commission on Law Enforcement and Administration of Justice (1967) suggested that "police departments in all communities with a substantial minority population must vigorously recruit minority police officers," that "the very presence of a predominantly White police force in a Negro community can serve as a dangerous irritant" (p. 167).

Though the task force report stressed that recruitment standards ought not to be compromised, it also pointed out that "certain selection standards may have the unintended effect of barring large numbers of minority group applicants who could adequately perform police work" (p. 171). As a case in point, the report noted the following:

> Young men who have grown up in poor, and particularly minority group, neighborhoods run a very great risk of acquiring a police record. In such circumstances, arrest records or conviction of a minor offense does not necessarily mean that the applicant is irresponsible or of poor character. . . . A minor record should be considered as part of an analysis of the moral character of the applicant based on all available information, rather than an automatic disqualification. (p. 171)

In 1965, the population of West Coast City was 23% Black, but the 750-man police department had only 16 Black officers. By dint of intensive recruitment, the minority representation had tripled by 1971, which was the date the no-confidence vote was taken. One would have thought that this achievement might be regarded by other officers as a positive result, but it instead surfaced as a complaint, with considerable emphasis on the issue of allegedly compromised hiring criteria:

> The chief has inaugurated a policy of hiring people with criminal records to work in the police department, both in a civilian and police officer capacity.
>
> [There is a] general lowering of qualifications for recruit officers hired in recent past; recruits [are] hired with juvenile records of felony violations.
>
> Under his leadership, department standards have been downgraded to the point where ex-felons are being hired as police officers.
>
> Supporting the policy of coaching and hiring substandard applicants, altering the written examination and requirements . . . allows substandard applicants to be hired in this day when the upgrading of policemen is demanded throughout the country.
>
> I feel that the new hiring procedures that have come about recently will in the future make [the department] a second-rate department.

By this, I mean the lowering of testing standards, backgrounds, and character standards of new recruits.

Unsurprisingly, complaints relating to the compromising of standards and the preferential treatment of minority officers were also voiced with respect to promotions and assignments. In this connection, the 1967 Task Force on the Police, President's Commission on Law Enforcement and Administration of Justice pointed out that "a police department should have several qualified higher ranking minority-group officers if it is to be responsive to the needs of minority neighborhoods" (p. 172). The West Coast City department had pursued this objective and managed to promote one of the Black officers to a senior leadership position.

The issue of a presumed selectivity of personnel assignments was variously broached in the no-confidence ballots:

> [The chief] is overly concerned with the Black officers in the department and will not give the same or equal amount of time and consideration to other officers in the department.

> He has continually transferred any minority member to various special assignments, almost always circumventing the appointee list. These minority members who receive special assignments are sometimes probationary members, and in one case, a minority member received a transfer who had never worked one single day on the street. . . . He is actually discriminating against White members. He should terminate non-sworn aides such as he recently employed.

> What would happen if we had a White officers association?

> A Negro can get any job in the department. . . . Why should the color of a person's skin make any difference to him?

> Discriminatory transfers . . . of one ethnic group into another division or section over other officers who have more seniority, experience, and have had their transfer letters in longer.

> He has conducted a scientific program of racism in reverse where minority officers are selected for the most desirable of jobs within the department.

If the goal of recruiting minority officers had been to capitalize on their enlightened attitudes and relevant backgrounds and experience by integrating the officers into the departmental culture, the goal of assimilation had remained unachieved. The Black officers were clearly able to contribute to the effectiveness of the department by enhancing its acceptance in the community, but they had to function as a self-contained enclave. The Black Officers Association evolved into one of several innovation ghettos allied with the chief and came to be regarded with envy and suspicion in the locker room.

POLICING THE POLICE

By far the most prevalent accusation lodged against the chief in 1971—as catalogued by the union representatives who had reviewed the ballots—was summarized as "Discipline: Too harsh and unfair." The source of the officers' displeasure had to do with the implementation of the kind of process of internal investigations, which according to the 1967 Task Force on the Police, President's Commission on Law Enforcement and Administration of Justice, "succeeds both in disciplining misbehaving officers and deterring others from misbehaving" (p. 194). According to the task force report,

> Once the department has obtained information concerning possible misconduct or violations of policies relating to community relations, it must give the same dedication and attention to further investigation and, when appropriate, punishment as it gives to other vital areas of police work. (p. 194)

Among the considerations that made such a policy particularly offensive from the average officer's perspective is that it violated the elementary assumption that the police are fundamentally the "good guys" and that they would have to retain that attribute despite any inconsequential lapses and insignificant foibles, which would have to be reasonably accommodated. One officer eloquently put it as follows:

> I feel that in his pursuit to ensure that "the old days" do not come back to haunt us, [the chief] has somehow forgotten that we are simply human beings susceptible to human frailties. We cannot

be programmed like computers and be expected to be wholly, totally, and completely error free. History bears evidence to only one flawless human being ever walking on this earth, and even he was crucified.

The other side of the equation was that criminal offenders were to be regarded as the "bad guys" and treated as such. Bad guys were to be subjected to a process of investigation and punishment, a process it would be inappropriate to apply to the good guys and that, when applied, would reduce their effectiveness in the pursuit of bad guys, which was the real object of the game.

Hence the unpopularity of the internal affairs division, which was the department's police-the-police entity and which had been strengthened and buttressed by the chief. The chief had also made it clear that all disciplinary decisions were ultimately his own to make, which nominated him as the plausible target of resentments:

> [The chief] seems more concerned about policing the police than policing the city, restraining the beatman and other personnel to the point they cannot effectively do a decent job.
>
> He enforces his policies by using his personal gestapo, internal affairs.
>
> [There is] extreme punishment for relatively minor offences, seemingly without taking into consideration a man's past accomplishments.
>
> Why is so much emphasis placed on sticking it to the officer when a complaint (as he likes to call them) is made? The complaint originally made may be unfounded, but if some minor report-writing error be found or he wasn't wearing a hat, etc., then it's Vaseline time for the officer.
>
> [The chief's] hard, fast rules on truthfulness and use of certain slurring words [makes me] feel oppressed.
>
> Officers have no backing and will not take actions on the streets anymore, which is not right in a large city.
>
> Many members who have been involved in disciplinary problems have been treated in a dehumanizing and unprofessional manner.

Patrolmen are constantly reminded directly and indirectly that we are racial bigots, graft takers, brutal, ignorant, and uneducated.

[Officers are given] 10 days off for using the word "Nigger"!

SOLICITING CITIZEN COMPLAINTS

From the citizens' perspective, a key element of a system of satisfactory police–community relations was to have some means available for seeking redress when one had been mistreated or brutalized by police officers. The usual vehicle for this purpose is a standardized procedure whereby citizens can file complaints and have them attended to. The Task Force on the Police, President's Commission on Law Enforcement and Administration of Justice (1967) postulated that "how a department treats [citizen] complaints is a general index of its concern or lack of concern for community relations" (p. 194).

In the past, many police departments had gone to extraordinary and imaginative lengths to make the filing of complaints as onerous and off-putting as possible. These departments could end up claiming that their data clearly demonstrated that they had no problems whatever in dealing with citizens, a contention that was patently fraudulent. By contrast, the West Coast City chief wanted the most accurate possible feedback from clients of police service and wanted to provide them reliable feedback in return. One way of achieving this goal was to facilitate the process of filing citizen complaints and to ensure that complaints were actually read and attended to.

The view expressed by the dissenting members who cast votes of no confidence in the chief was that he had gone much too far with his hospitability, especially by allowing citizens to file anonymous complaints. Many officers seemed to be asking whose side the chief was on:

His policy of instructing Internal Affairs to investigate anonymous complaints is ridiculous.

Even a criminal has a right to face his accusers.

[He was] encouraging people to make reports against officers, where the officer has no chance to confront the person making the complaint.

When a citizen complains it is necessary for the patrolman to prove beyond a reasonable doubt that he acted correctly.

[He is] always soliciting complaints of the populace against policemen. This chief never fights for the men.

Internal Affairs should be reorganized and should investigate only signed complaints made in person. False reports should be prosecuted.

If he would concern himself less with protecting the "constitutional rights" of every "donkey" on the street and think more of protecting his men, things would be much better.

He has publicly and privately asked subversive groups to make complaints against police. . . . Even criminals get a second chance.

Speaking of "criminals" who "get a second chance," many of the officers indicated on their ballots that they were voting to oust the chief because he had issued an order forbidding the shooting of fleeing burglars, which had been the prevailing practice in West Coast City.[6] Some of the officers also felt that the chief had cemented his status as an enemy of law and order by issuing guidelines to discourage the promiscuous use of field interceptions and interrogations (see Chapter 10, this volume). The 1967 Task Force on the Police, President's Commission on Law Enforcement and Administration of Justice mentioned the department's guidelines to support the general proposition that "to balance the need for field interrogations and the harmful effect on police community relations which may result from their indiscriminate use . . . police departments should adopt detailed policies governing this authority" (p. 185). As an example of such a policy, the task force proposed that "field interrogations should not be used at all for minor crimes like vagrancy and loitering" (p. 185).[7]

---

[6] The chief's policy with respect to the shooting of fleeing burglars has become a universal rule in police departments today and is no longer controversial.

[7] In an amazing exercise in clairvoyance, the Task Force on the Police, President's Commission on Law Enforcement and Administration of Justice (1967) anticipated today's headlines with the following prescription:

Officers should be required to file a report each time a stop is made in order to record the circumstances and persons involved. Even greater care should be taken with these records, than with arrest records so that the police do not use them to establish the delinquency or bad character of the person stopped. Moreover, the records identifying suspects should not be available to persons outside of public law enforcement agencies. (p. 185)

With respect to anonymous citizen complaints, Samuel Walker (2005) pointed out that they are nowadays frequently required by consent decrees following litigation. However, he argued:

> Whether or not to accept anonymous complaints depends on how one views the complaint process. If it is narrowly defined as analogous to the criminal process, with the goal of adjudicating guilt or innocence, then it follows that complaints should be signed. But if complaints are viewed as management information that helps a department proactively address potential performance problems, then it makes sense to accept anonymous complaints. The latter view has emerged as the new standard and has been incorporated in most of the settlements negotiated by the U.S. Department of Justice. (p. 78)

Irrespective of which definition one had elected to apply to the goal of the process in the 1960s (and the distinction was probably not watertight at the time), some aggrieved residents of West Coast City must have appreciated the unprecedented opportunity to file complaints with few bureaucratic restraints and without fear of repercussions.

THE POLICE CHIEF AS CHANGE AGENT

The West Coast City police chief belonged to a category of police administrators who are formally tasked as change agents. In the sixties, these reform chiefs or commissioners were appointed with the expectation— or at minimum, the hope—that they could do something to ameliorate the resentment that had been engendered in minority communities by insensitive police practices. This mandate made police officers the targets of reform, and some of the officers more of a target than others. As a result, one would expect that overaggressive, interpersonally inept, or racially prejudiced officers might end up feeling vulnerable, an eventuality that would not cause much loss of sleep among dedicated reformers.

However, surgical circumscriptions in the locker room are almost impossible to effect. For one, what with the high value assigned to solidarity in the peer culture, any threat or accusation aimed at any member of the force is liable to be perceived as a threat by others. For another, individual officers who become targets of change would have to be defensibly selected, and lines between offensive behavior and inoffensive behavior are often difficult to draw. And where judgmental distinctions are incontestably clear-cut—such as with reliably documented differences between corrupt and noncorrupt officers or between officers who are habitually overaggressive and others—the criteria that are used may appear negotiable to self-defined pragmatic practitioners, who pride themselves in the fond presumption that they are attuned to the peremptory "realities" of the streets.

Last, there is the matter of top-down change, which tends to invite bottom-up resistance. In police departments, a special feeling of betrayal can be engendered by actions of top administrators that are perceived to be rejecting and punitive. These feelings tend to be personalized because police hierarchies are typically headed by all-powerful leaders who are expected by officers to offer them backing and support. Given the centralization of power (presumably enacted as insurance against political interference), the top positions in police organizations—those of chief or commissioner—are often experienced by subordinates as quasi-parental, which invites emotionally loaded responses. Even under ordinary circumstances, police officers tend to express ambivalence about their top leadership, with a commingling of feelings of dependence and circumscription. However, ambivalence becomes easily transmuted into resentment where the dependency needs of officers are not met, or a sense of parental rejection is mobilized. This is the sort of transmutation that psychoanalysts have labeled *transference,* because the response appears disproportionate to the occasion.[8] In the case of West Coast City officers, feelings of abandonment often surfaced in person-centered comments about the chief that were appended to no-confidence votes:

> How can police officers look up to a chief who looks down on them?
>
> I feel that he shows no compassion for the men of the department.
>
> He will not acknowledge the fact that you exist, should you run into him in the hall, street, or elevator.

---

[8] The term applies to occasions when responses to a person or situation are magnified or distorted by association with emotionally vested past relationships.

[The chief] shows no interest in the welfare of his men and cannot relate to his men, especially [those] in uniform.

The man has to my knowledge never been around to talk with the "troops." He appears to go out of his way to avoid ever saying hello to his fellow officers.

This man is not human—[he] shows no compassion or feeling.

Feelings about the messenger of reform ultimately merge with feelings about the message of reform. Across the board, the community-relations approach that was being promoted by the reformist chiefs came to be perceived by the rank and file as a hostile assault from above, which had to be vigorously and self-protectively resisted. This widely shared determination led to the birth (or rebirth) of militant police unions in many large cities. This union movement combined traditional concerns about bread-and-butter issues with reactionary ideological positions and virulent and acrimonious opposition to local police leadership. The unions could not unseat police chiefs by sponsoring no-confidence votes, but they ultimately contributed to developments that limited the power of chiefs to unilaterally enact reforms. Samuel Walker (1998) pointed out the following:

> By the mid-1970s, most big-city departments outside the South were operating under collective bargaining agreements . . . drastically reducing the power of police chiefs and giving the rank and file a voice in many important decisions. Due process provisions of union contracts gave officers tremendous protection against arbitrary disciplinary actions. Some observers believed that unionism spelled the death of police reform, since professionalization had relied on strong chiefs. (p. 200)[9]

Unions countered the management effort to control the actions of the rank and file with negotiated counter rules to circumscribe the actions of management. The combined force field gave birth to a variety of new arrangements and new ways of responding to the concerns of officers and members of the community.

---

[9] Walker (1998) also noted that although unions "opposed many innovations, particularly programs designed to improve police–community relations, the unions won substantial improvements in salaries and benefits that helped make policing a more attractive career" (p. 200).

SEATTLE, 2010–2011

6

The Birth of Modern Policing

The sixties were an unsettling time for hard-charging police officers who had come to expect compliance—or at least a show of acquiescence—from the citizenry and encouragement or supportive neglect from their superiors. The testimonials I sampled in Chapter 2 through Chapter 4 reflect the pained surprise of officers who found that they had to increasingly deal with unwelcome interference and expressions of resentment from crowds of unfriendly spectators. The situation was equally discouraging when the officers returned to the locker room. The rebellion I sampled in Chapter 5 illustrates the discouragement and the feeling of having been abandoned and thrown to the encircling wolves.

In the face of resentments from the rank and file, reform chiefs found themselves increasingly relying on constituencies in the community for support. Because many of these constituencies (especially in the late sixties) were not noted for their admiration of the police, these efforts cemented questions in the ranks about whose side the chief was on, on top of other charges, such as those related to affirmative-action hiring, sponsorship of "social work," indifference to crime, sadistic management, cold heartedness, and disloyalty to subordinates.

Though it was not obvious, reform chiefs could count on some measure of support within their organization, beyond the enthusiastic backing of the Black Officers Association and that of resident social scientists working on federal grants. There were times when even the hardest-charging officers (such as our interview subjects) might have found themselves expressing grudging admiration for one or another community-oriented project:

P27:[1] Well, [West Coast City] has a policy—I don't know if any other department has it—it's called a citizenship program where we take let's say, juvenile offenders or even adult offenders of very, very minor misdemeanors—even traffic violations—and we send them to a school, maybe 2 nights for 2 hours, and we try to teach these people what good citizenship requires. Like I say, I don't know if any other department does this, and I think this system is good, except that the people don't go, or 2 hours isn't enough to tell them anything.[2]

Some officers also recalled becoming individually involved in efforts to broker or mobilize social services on behalf of disadvantaged citizens (e.g., neglected children), though they would not think of defining such activities as community oriented or as social work:

P5: The other day I made a report on these children. These children live in a second story apartment house and momma was gone, and she had eight children. Well, momma was going with every Tom, Dick, and Harry in the neighborhood. Well, the children were left in the house unattended—no one there to take care of them, no food in the house. . . . They were spraying water into the house next door . . . so a lot of officers say, "Just quit that," and go on their way. Well, what I did, I made a report. . . . And I said, "Either their welfare worker is inadequate, or she doesn't know her job." I don't know whether she liked that or not,

---

[1] Numbers again indicate different officers who were numbered sequentially in the original study.

[2] The two excepts on this page are from incident-centered interviews conducted under the auspices of the police department, with the support and sponsorship from the National Institute of Mental Health (NIMH) Center for the Study of Crime and Delinquency.

but it's right in the report, because she wasn't doing her job. She wasn't doing her job at all. I mean, it was apparent. No food in the house, a boy friend taking care of the kids. The oldest was 11 and there were eight of them. That's a lot of kids.

Many chiefs of the period created special units to broaden the mandates of their organizations by delivering services to citizens. West Coast City, for example, fielded an experimental family crisis unit to adjudicate family disputes, and a group that helped tenants who were being summarily evicted by their landlords. Enterprises such as these were typically staffed by officers who had volunteered for their assignments and were philosophically aligned with their community-oriented chiefs. As a matter of course, unit members were therefore frequently looked down on by their peers, who were not shy about expressing their disapproval. The result was that special units frequently became innovation ghettos embedded in an impervious and change-resistant culture.

The most prominent special units fielded during this period were police-community-relations units, which were independently created in several large police departments, with the mandate to serve different segments of the community. These units were invariably described by their peers as not engaged in police work.[3] Reiss (1985) noted the following:

> What was cloudy at the beginning became transparent with time—
> that police–community relationships could not be manufactured by
> assigning responsibility for them to a group of officers in a special-
> ized public relations unit. Nor did it help much to put minority
> officers in such specialized units when most policing is done by a tra-
> ditional police cadre. The lesson to be gained from those ventures in
> police–community relations was that a chief cannot affect relation-
> ships between the citizens and police personnel by bureaucratically
> specializing responsibility for them. (pp. 61–62)

---

[3] The hostility against such units is exemplified by the break between the San Francisco Community Relations Unit and the rest of the force which eventuated when members of the unit were alleged to initiate complaints involving other officers.

THE ADVENT OF COMMUNITY-ORIENTED POLICING

Police–community relations became the mother lode of enlightened police reform. A transitional development involved experimentation with a decentralized arrangement of generalist units that functioned as mini-police departments within police departments. This arrangement was called *team policing*, and it "vested power in autonomous groups of officers who were accorded responsibility for providing police service to a neighborhood or community" (Toch & Grant, 2005, p. 41). Team policing came to represent a revolution because "a corollary was that the groups of officers would work closely with residents in defining their self-assigned missions" (Toch & Grant, 2005, p. 41).

Team policing as such did not survive, mostly because tensions invariably developed as a result of jurisdictional disputes. However, the precedent of providing citizens with opportunities to be listened to and to help shape the content of police services not only survived but also prospered. As the idea gained traction, it ended up taking different forms in the course of its advertised implementation, and some of these were more tangible than others. The entire range of actual and ostensible efforts to offer citizens the opportunity to provide input and to have their views taken into account has come to be known as *community-oriented policing*.

CONCERN WITH QUALITY OF LIFE PROBLEMS

Citizens may never be of one mind in their definition of priorities, but they do usually deviate from traditional police practices and predilections. Thus, Wesley Skogan (2008) reported:

> At the public meetings held every month all over the city [of Chicago], residents complain about teen loitering, graffiti, noise, and loose garbage in the alleys. . . . They also express a great deal of concern about abandoned cars, rats running loose in the alleyways, dilapidated buildings, homeless people sleeping in the parks, missing street signs, burned-out street lights, and runaway youths squatting in abandoned buildings. (p. 30)

Such complaints focus on quality of life, which the average hard-charging police officer would never nominate as his dominant concern. A farcical reconciliation can be (and has been) effected by formulating as a police objective arresting nuisance offenders. This transmutation (which sells traditional policing under the guise of community policing) has been called the *broken windows approach* and rests on the assumption that quality-of-life transgressions call for crime fighting, because they are a prelude to more serious crime. But even if there was evidence for some sort of progression from public disorder to mainline criminality, preemptively arresting penny-ante offenders (e.g., chronic alcoholic itinerants, homeless persons snoozing on park benches) would be a wildly inappropriate approach. It would not only be unkind to persons who by and large are already disadvantaged, but it would also serve to criminalize behavior that could be far more effectively addressed by social agencies other than the police.

Once this point is recognized, the goal of the enterprise changes from arresting penny-ante malefactors to mobilizing resources that can ameliorate the situations that happen to be of priority concern to the citizens. Because these situations (e.g., abandoned cars cluttering up the neighborhood, defective street lighting, open-air drug bazaars that conduct business under people's living room windows) tend to be a heterogeneous conglomerate, a variety of solutions might have to be mobilized to address them.

The first order of business would be to define the cluster of situations at issue, which constitute the problem to be addressed. Given the nature of this task, the approach has been called *problem-oriented policing* and has come to represent another addition to the taxonomy of police-community-relations reforms.

LEARNING TO ACCOMMODATE REFORM

The rank and file of police departments have had to live with the language of these and other reformist approaches—which was typically embedded in refurbished mission statements—and have largely done so on the assumption that community-oriented proclamations need carry no implication for the business of crime fighting on the streets. In this expectation, the officers could count on support from conservative middle managers and line supervisors, who frequently suggested in lineups that police chiefs tend to come and go, as do their politically motivated interventions.[4] Many community groups also became hotbeds of cynicism and contended that in the past good intentions had never produced tangible results, so why consider wasting time attending newly advertised meetings with police?

Some activists in the community were reliably even more hostile because they were accustomed to categorizing the police as systemically racist and congenitally violence prone. Their perspective tended to gain traction whenever encounters between citizens and officers degenerated into messy conflict situations. Skogan (2008) thus noted:

> There is evidence that the seemingly endless recurrence of highly publicized acts of police violence affects public attitudes, reversing occasional improvements in public opinion. Community policing promises that police will accommodate the public and not just the other way around. However, when use of excessive force or killings by police becomes a public issue, years of progress in police–community relations can disappear. (p. 32)

Skogan (2008) observed that "nasty misconduct . . . diverts attention of the media from the unnewsworthy aspects of police reform" (p. 32). This tendentiousness was reinforced in the sixties by the chorus, which drew media attention to "nasty misconduct" by pointing to its occurrence.

THE AUGMENTATION OF THE CHORUS

We now turn to recent developments that show that this capacity to garner media attention has been significantly augmented and that, as a result, the border between the chorus and the media's coverage of nasty misconduct has been largely obfuscated and obliterated. In the process, we should be observing substantial differences between the past and present

---

[4] Many community-oriented programs have been introduced under direct auspices of police chiefs and police commissioners, bypassing most of the intervening layers of the hierarchy, with the result that middle managers have often felt excluded.

as a result of changes that have involved both the police and the community. However, we shall also note surprising commonalities, which may serve to illustrate the fact that the history of police reform has turned out to be more cumulative than linear. In other words, the past—as we sampled it in Part I of this book—may still be with us and has come to be overlaid rather than supplanted by ensuing efforts to overcome it.

The transmutation of the chorus into what it has become today began modestly, with isolated incidents in which questionable arrests by police officers were memorialized by amateur photographers who serendipitously had cameras pointed in the requisite direction. Some of the bystanders ended up making their films available to local television stations, which disseminated the scenarios to the predictable surprise and consternation of the authorities and the officers involved. By far the most fateful of these filmed incidents was the beating of Rodney King by members of the Los Angeles Police Department. This horrendous scenario has been described as "perhaps the most widely publicized incident involving the use of force in modern history" (Vila & Morris, 1999, p. 266). The repercussions may have been far from inevitable: The Rodney King tape was initially offered to the police, but a desk sergeant rejected the offer as of no particular interest.[5] Manning (2003) captured the historical importance of the Rodney King incident:

> Perhaps it is obvious that the King beating was natural activity converted into a televised event. . . . It apparently fits the reality rules that enable viewers to see a brief video as an instance of real events and become outraged and active. By seeing this video as real and embedded in the course of events, viewers endowed television reality with political power. The film surely had a mobilizing or rallying point function in the May 1992 Los Angeles riots. (p. 243)

---

[5] Some of the sergeants' superiors were also underwhelmed. Daryl Gates, the chief of the Los Angeles Police Department, commented: "Any depiction of force can appear worse than it is." Polls, however, showed that virtually all respondents in post-Rodney King surveys felt that the amount of force depicted in the tape had been wildly excessive. Flanagan and Vaughn (1996) concluded from survey data of the period that "studies on police use of force taken in their totality indicated that some portion of the high level of perceived police brutality is probably due to the extraordinary media attention given to the King incident" (p. 124).

In the wake of technological changes that have resulted in the widespread availability of inexpensive videotaping equipment, it has eventually become commonplace for police officers to discover that their involvements are being recorded and disseminated. In such instances, the chorus is no longer circumscribed by the spectators immediately present at the scene. Outrage and indignation, protest and recrimination, can now be mobilized on an unfettered scale, free of geographical boundaries and physical constraints.

Early on, some police officials saw risk, and others potential, in these developments. The issue of perceived risk (whose invocation sometimes bordered on paranoia) was by far the more salient. Individual officers frequently argued that the threat of publicity could place them in danger, and a number of publicized incidents occurred in which police officers arrested amateur photographers, invoking charges such as disturbing the peace, provoking a riot, resisting arrest, or endangering the officer. The most fashionable gambit had been to rely on statutes that prohibit eavesdropping. McElroy (2010) pointed out the following:

> In at least three states, it is now illegal to record any on-duty police officer. . . . Illinois, Massachusetts, and Maryland are among the 12 states in which all parties must consent for a recording to be legal. . . . Since the police do not consent, the camera wielder can be arrested. (para. 1–3)

Where the camera wielder is arrested, the question of police brutality tends to be refocused from the incident that is being filmed to the arrest of the spectator who has introduced the question. In the transposed scenario, the officer who has done the arresting becomes the villain of the piece for one constituency, whereas he is seen as acting in righteous self-defense by another.

A young couple in Rochester, New York, recently videotaped a traffic stop in front of their house and were asked to move by an officer but declined to do so. They then videotaped their degenerating encounter with the officer:

> For more than a minute of the video, the officer and Good [the female camera wielder] argue about whether she is threatening his safety.

> Finally, it appears, [the officer] has had enough: "You know what, you're gonna go to jail. That's just not right." (Sledge, 2011, para. 15)

As reported in a subsequent newspaper story, "Good's arrest became a viral sensation after the video of her arrest was posted on YouTube.com. . . . [and] the media attention elevated the misdemeanor arrest, prompting the police department to scrutinize its own activities" (Craig, 2011, pp. 3–4). Along the way, various news releases and publicized appearances by opposing protagonists (including by union representatives who had charged in a police blog that officers were being threatened by militant activists) provoked virulent responses from the chorus, ranging from "How about just taking the video and beating the crap out of her in an alley" ("Officers Threatened," 2011, Member Comments section) and "She's a stupid liberal hippy bitch . . . [who] makes me want to vomit" (Kimbrough, 2011, p. 1) to "Cops are punks with badges" (ridoshi2117, 2011, Comments section) and "This woman risked her own safety, even her own life in order to do what Martin Luther King would have praised her for" (ridoshi2117, 2011, Comments section).

McElroy (2010) observed the following:

> When the police act as though cameras were the equivalent of guns pointed at them, there is a sense in which they are correct. Cameras have become the most effective weapon that ordinary people have to protect against and to expose police abuse. (para. 20)

But as it happens, the same source of information can be immensely useful to reform administrators of progressive police departments and to police officers who need to counter false and malicious accusations. In fact, it has become commonplace for police cars to be equipped with dashboard cameras so that incidents can be recorded and reviewed.

CHORUS AMPLIFICATION

The first step in the inception of a chorus still occurs when some members of a crowd decide that the proceedings they are witnessing are of more than passing interest. In other words, some of the spectators conclude that the scenario they are observing has news value, in the sense that other persons who are not present at the scene might find the information of interest or of concern. If they act on this inference and it turns out to be correct, this can lead to the formation of a chorus among interested parties who are not present at the scene. Such a chorus can be considered to be largely a "virtual chorus" because it is a chorus of absentees. In the more conventional sequence, chorus formation begins with partisan spectators who feel the need to draw other people's attention to the encounter they are witnessing because they favor one set of the participants or, more to the point, because they object to the actions of others. Chorus formation can also be initiated by a participant in the confrontation, such as a friend or relative of the citizen who is the target of police attention.

A chorus opens at whatever juncture feelings about the proceedings at issue are publicly expressed. Eventually, opinions that are publicly expressed reflect different sets of feelings of different sets of spectators, with the feelings of persons at any given stage of the process being ratified, endorsed, or responded to by those of persons at a subsequent stage. This sequence is cumulative, in the sense that successive waves of respondents add voices to the chorus. But this numerical reinforcement does not mean that the result need be harmonious: Most choral presentations of consequence are likely to become messy, in that some of the feelings that are expressed are apt to invite a response from persons with divergent or opposing feelings.

Many public police–citizen confrontations are likely to attract crowds of spectators today just as they did decades ago (see Chapters 2 through 4, this volume). On average, however, the level of acrimony among these spectators has become attenuated, in that there is no longer much of a threat of chorus members turning into riot participants. Instead, today's bystanders tend to appear at the scene heavily armed with recording equipment. This means that if a gadget-armed spectator decides to share his or her experience, he or she can e-mail at warp speed a segment of the action to anyone who has another cell phone or available computer. Most scenarios that are thus transmitted testify to the endemic nature of this behavior because they are apt to depict fellow spectators recording the same incident from different directions for varying periods of time.

DISSEMINATION AND NETWORK FORMATION

The scenarios that are recorded by spectators of police–citizen encounters tend to be shared with persons whom the spectators know and find personally or ideologically congenial. These recipients may in turn have soul mates who they feel might be interested in police–citizen confrontations, especially police–citizen confrontations that are likely to make them angry. This second cohort of recipients may have another cohort of congenial and like-minded friends. Over time (which can be instantaneous), such a distribution chain can end up with an ad hoc network with shared views that doubles as a chorus segment.

Network creation can be formalized if a spectator is young at heart and belongs to a social network or instant-messaging arrangement. Network creation is likely to be further facilitated if a spectator is an activist affiliated with a civic organization or special interest group. If the group or organization to which the spectator belongs decides that the police incident can serve as grist for its agenda, it can instantaneously relay the scenario to the media (which by this time may have already received copies from other spectators) to ensure the widest possible dissemination of helpful information.

The media nowadays form a large multifaceted conglomerate. The category of "media" comprises not only traditional venues, such as newspapers and television channels, but also their Internet extensions and supplements. In addition, a large and diverse assortment of professional and amateur blogs is being offered through the Internet. Many of these blogs focus on public policy, including issues related to criminal justice.[6]

Many professional blogs have a steady and loyal following that adds up to a network or a set of networks. Some blogs have limited-access arrangements, but most are available for public consumption. Not only blogs but also most Internet-based media invite comments from their readers. When large numbers of persons respond to such an invitation, the result can be an overwhelming chorus. In such a chorus, when opinionated members

---

[6] One prominent blog, for example, is called *Police Issues* (http://www.policeissues.com) and provides in-depth coverage of police-related issues.

respond to others with whose views they disagree, the vociferous chorus is apt to become unpleasantly cacophonous. The Internet is a medium that can readily deliver a *clamorous chorus:* a response with such volume and intensity that it becomes impossible for a police department or other target to ignore.

CLAMOROUS CHORUS FORMATION

Clamorous chorus formation can occur in relation to any social stimulus that elicits feelings of indignation among an appreciable number of people. Depictions of police violence may rank high on the hierarchy of such scenarios, but closer to the top of the list is the witnessing of animal abuse. A classic sequence of this kind recently unfolded in England, where

> Lola the cat was discovered unhappily yowling in a garbage bin outside the home of [its] owners. . . . In hopes of discovering who had trashed kitty, the [owners] looked at secure footage of the area, which showed an unidentified middle aged woman petting the cat, and then dropping it in the trash. The couple posted the video online, naturally, in an attempt to find out who the woman was. (Ehrlich, 2010, para. 3)

The "middle-aged woman" perpetrator was in due course identified and was transmuted into the most hated woman in the world, according to the press. The security video that featured her transgression was posted on YouTube, and in short order accumulated 350,000 views. Facebook groups were shortly "founded to bash [the perpetrator, and] one page raked in more that 6,700 fans" (Sheridan, 2010, para. 9). A particularly enthusiastic group had to be deleted because it suggested that the woman be lynched.

Individual comments that were posted to blogs reflected comparable sentiments. One person, for example, opined, "If I had seen her doing this to my cat I would have beaten her to within an inch of her life. I would have made sure that **** would never walk again" (Snead, 2010, Comments section). Another concerned person speculated, "Maybe stick her in a garbage can for a few hours and see how she likes it" (Snead, 2010,

Comments section). And a third person venomously asserted, "This chick is so fat, old, and ugly we should throw her out with the rubbish" ("Cat Put In Wheelie Bin," 2010, Comments section). (This being England, some comments were more understated, such as a suggestion that the woman might be more of a dog person or the suggestion that she might be emotionally disturbed and thus deserve treatment rather than a death sentence.)

The local authorities responded to the chorus by initiating what they characterized as an exhaustive investigation and raising the possibility of a criminal prosecution. There were also repercussions at the woman's place of employment. Customers of the bank where she worked as a cashier talked of initiating a boycott. Some submitted observations such as "I'd never be served by this despicable woman" (Trowbridge, 2010, para. 7) and "It's shocking that somebody you trust with your money and you think leads a respectable life can do something like this" (Trowbridge, 2010, para. 8). Unsurprisingly, the bank's managers announced that "the matter" would be taken "very seriously" (Trowbridge, 2010, para. 6).

WITNESSING POLICE INTERVENTIONS

In the next three chapters (Chapters 7 through 9) we delineate a sequence of events that transpired over a period of several months, involving responses of a contemporary chorus—a chorus of spectators that mobilized the media, which mobilized additional spectators—to several controversial encounters between police officers and citizens in Seattle.

The Seattle Police Department provides an interesting parallel to that of West Coast City in that it also served as a target of community-oriented reform. S. Herbert (2006) thus noted the following:

> In the 1990s, the Seattle Police Department attempted an ambitious reform effort. Under the leadership of Chief Norm Stamper . . . the department tried to reorient all of its operations around the philosophy of community policing. For Stamper, this meant making the police an agency through which myriad efforts at neighborhood betterment

could be channeled. The police would listen closely to a wide range of citizen complaints, and would address as many of them as possible. . . . The mandate was deliberately broad: It was to be the linchpin agency in neighborhood efforts at self-improvement. (p. 94)

S. Herbert (2006) also pointed out that Chief Stamper's proposals generally met with vociferous and cynical resistance in the locker room.[7] However, the ideas he managed to introduce (and some counterpart developments in the community) facilitated actions by subsequent administrations that were designed to enhance the responsiveness of the department to the citizens of Seattle. These reform efforts included an advertised interest in feedback from the public, which encompassed the published observations of interested spectators to police–citizen encounters. Such receptivity carries obvious risk where adverse feedback cumulates because a series of incidents have invited unfavorable reviews.

---

[7] Stamper's predecessor, Chief Fitzsimmons, headed the Department from 1977 through 1994. During this hefty period of time, a number of reforms had been enacted to improve the department's tarnished reputation, including the successful hiring of minority officers, the dissemination of foot patrol, and the establishment of community police teams in 1990 "to closely interact with the community to resolve neighborhood problems and concerns through the use of traditional and nontraditional police tactics and the coordinated application of resources beyond those available within the criminal justice system" (Seattle Police Department document, cited in Lyons, 1999, p. 127).

A Video Clip in Seattle

On June 15, 2010, a television station in Seattle (KING 5 News) aired a videotape of an incident that showed, according to the station, "a veteran [police] officer throwing a punch at a 17-year-old girl, landing on her chin" (Romero & Forman, 2010, para. 2). The station's news release mentioned that "as a crowd of people gathered around the officer and teens, a man who heard them argue pulled out his camera and videotaped the incident. He later distributed the tape to local media" (Romero & Forman, 2010, para. 11).

The following detailed record of the confrontation appeared in *The Seattle Times* the same day and cited accounts released by the police:

> Walsh [the officer], working in a patrol car, saw several people jay-walking . . . despite a nearby pedestrian overpass.
>
> Walsh tried to stop a group of females when one woman, later identified as Levias, began walking away, according to an incident report.
>
> Walsh told Levias she must identify herself so he could issue her a citation or she would face arrest for obstruction, the report said.

Levias continued to walk away, prompting Walsh to grab her upper arm with his right hand, the report said.

At that point, Levias said something like "get the [expletive] off me," tensed her body and began to resist, the report said.

Walsh placed her upper body on the hood of his patrol car in trying to handcuff her. Levias began twisting around and pulled away, ignoring Walsh's command to stop resisting as she continued to struggle with him.

While Walsh tried to handcuff Levias, Rosenthal, the 17-year-old, approached Walsh, grabbing and pushing him. Walsh responded by punching Rosenthal. . . . During the incident, a hostile crowd of onlookers gathered and appeared to be cheering Levias and Rosenthal, the police report said. (Miletich & Sullivan, 2010, June 15, para. 22–29)

The entire sequence of events had been videotaped by one of the bystanders, who described his interest as commercial. The man said he had for years "walked around Seattle with a camcorder around his neck looking for some action . . . [to] maybe earn a few bucks selling the footage" (O'Hagan, 2010, para. 1). He said that some of his past recorded adventures had been "posted on You Tube until the site shut him down. They included fights, accidents, even a guy who pulled a knife and tried to kill himself" (O'Hagan, 2010, para. 7). In retrospect, the man modestly observed, "I guess I'm kind of at the right spot at the right time" (O'Hagan, 2010, para. 9).

Although this bystander's interests appeared to be nonpartisan, the same could not be said of other spectators who concurrently filmed the incident, nor of the first spokespersons who elected to respond to it. These commentators at times appeared heavily predisposed to question the motivation of the officer and to prejudge the officer's culpability:

> "This is another case of we are standing here and we are saying to the police shame on you," said James Kelly, president and CEO of the Urban League. . . . "[The officer] escalated a situation that could have turned into a riot there," said Chris Bennett, *Seattle Medium* founder. (Romero & Forman, 2010, para. 4–5)

> "At this time our community seems to be in an abusive relationship with law enforcement," says Seattle/King County NAACP [National

Association for the Advancement of Colored People] president James Bible. "We're living in a hostile environment for people of color, and a hostile environment for people in poverty." . . . "This was an appalling act of injustice," said pastor Reggie Witherspoon of Mt. Calvary Christian Center. "There is no way it can be looked at as proper behavior and we are demanding that something be done about it." (Bennett, 2010, para. 15–18)

Subsequent statements tended to be more moderate, acknowledging that blame might not be easy to allocate, given all of the resisting and intervening and wrestling and subduing that seemed to be going on, or pointing out that maybe judgment ought to be deferred until all the facts were in. The Seattle Police Department predictably opted for the latter position:

Acting Deputy Chief Nick Metz, speaking at a hastily called news conference Tuesday morning, expressed concerns about Walsh's conduct, saying the department was "withholding judgment" pending a separate internal investigation into the officer's action by the department's civilian-led Office of Civilian Responsibility. . . . Metz said he contacted leaders of Seattle's African–American community Monday night, telling them that an investigation would be conducted. (Miletich & Sullivan, 2010, June 15, para. 6, 13)

THE UNION'S RESPONSE

The details of the videotaped encounter have a great deal in common with incidents described by the West Coast City officers in the sixties (see Chapters 2–4, this volume), including the interventions of—and physical confrontations with—partisan spectators. The parallel is sufficiently striking to allow for questions about differences (if any) in the way the incidents in these widely separated periods were responded to. Chief Metz alluded to one relevant variable: the attention to the internal investigation and the question of whether the process would end up being regarded as fair and/or dispassionate by members of the community. A related question was whether trust would be accorded to the process by the police department's rank and file and its union(s). (See Chapter 5, this volume.)

The union that represents Seattle officers—including sergeants—
is the Police Officers' Guild, which has some 1,250 members. The guild's
president, Rich O'Neill, initially defended Officer Walsh, commenting that
Walsh had, if anything, been overly restrained in countering the provocations
to which he was subjected:

> O'Neill said the officer reacted the way he was trained, and the only
> reason the situation escalated was because of the alleged violators'
> actions. He repeated one question: Why didn't they comply?
>
> "Let's put the accountability where it needs to be. They [the teens]
> escalated the situation.
>
> "You escalate a situation when you put your hands on a uniformed
> officer—you have no reason to do that," O'Neill said. "There's no
> justification to ever do that. And when you make that decision to go
> down that road then the officer is going to resort to their training."
> (McNerthney, 2010, June 14, para. 13–15)

The union's president dismissed the relevance of the citizen's gender
(citing examples of ferocious females) and of race ("gets old after a while";
McNerthney, 2010, June 14, p. 2). However, he went on to express confidence in the department's internal review, pointing out that "if the officer
treats you poorly, we have an accountability system that's multitiered,
and you can make a complaint, and that complaint will be addressed"
(McNerthney, 2010, June 14, p. 2). This position is amazingly discrepant
from the distrust and cynicism of the West Coast City union representatives.
It is inconceivable that West Coast City's militant union representatives
would have favored any contacts with community groups, as did President
O'Neill, who said that "good things happen when people are talking to
each other" (McNerthney, 2010, June 14, p. 2). And given the anti-chief
revolt delineated in Chapter 5, it is surprising and revealing that O'Neill
issued a statement in which he praised the acting (and future) chief of his
department, noting that the chief "has [demonstrated] that he can lead a
very large department through the worst of times. . . . [and thus] has the
proven experience in leading a large urban police force" (McNerthney, 2010,
June 17, para. 9).

In the sixties, we encountered substantial divergence between the positions of traditional and minority police unions. In Seattle, the difference in views that emerged was between the responses of two minority unions: the National Black Police Association and its Seattle (Washington state) affiliate. Although the national organization cited Officer Walsh's actions as "an example of excessive force," suggesting that the Seattle department had made its hiring decisions without adequate personality-related screening (Cooper, 2010, para. 2), the Washington union stood squarely behind Officer Walsh and asserted that "as regrettable as it looks, the officer used great restraint in dealing with the female that pushed him. He maintained a professional demeanor while in an adverse and potentially volatile situation" ("Black Police Organizations," 2010, para. 8). Both organizations went on record as favoring training related to the appropriate use of force, and neither group saw the videotaped incident as race related.

THE VOICES OF THE CHORUS

Within hours after the original encounter it would have been impossible to find anyone in the greater Seattle area who had not repeatedly seen the videotape, which had been included in every local newscast. Various versions of the video had also been featured in Internet reports and widely publicized in blogs of every conceivable description, across the country and abroad. In several of these venues, viewers had been invited to respond. On June 18, 2010, for example, a news-oriented source (Martinez, 2010, on CBS News.com) asked its readers, "Were the cop's actions justified or was it police brutality?" Responses included the following:

- She was asking for it. . . . She's just lucky she didn't get tasered.
- She should have listened to him. The officer did what he had to do.
- This is a complicated situation. I don't know who's right.
- The punch seems like too much. The cop should be put on leave.
- Punched in the face for jaywalking?!? The cop should be the one in jail.

After a period, this query elicited some 50 entries, with many comments addressed to other comments with whom the author(s) disagreed. There were also critical observations about perceived deficiencies of the survey. To the extent to which the comments were responsive, most of them defended the actions of the officer on the ground that it is a serious transgression to assault a police officer.

It would be impossible to classify and tabulate every single comment made in response to each news story on this issue. However, a rough sampling suggests that although most respondents had concluded that race in this case was not relevant as a variable,[1] most felt it appropriate to focus on age, expressing concerns about the upbringing and resulting deportment of undisciplined adolescents, with the perpetrators as an obvious case in point. (It may have helped in this regard that coverage of the original incident included highlights from the checkered history of both girls.)

Very few of the commentators responding to the story on CBS.com took the occasion to attack or indict the Seattle Police Department, a sentiment originally expressed by a handful of community activists. The closest thing to a critique in some of the comments had to do with the disproportionate use of police resources to control and to penalize jaywalking. It is most significant that no questions were raised about the readiness or capability of the police department to respond to citizen concerns or complaints.

As for the original group of spectators—the persons who pioneered the chorus formation—a blog based in Kansas City pointed out that the crowd appeared to be unfriendly to Officer Walsh but was restrained in its responses. The officer had been put on notice by spectators, however, that his actions were being recorded:

> This was a White cop engaging in physical contact with two Black females. It had the potential to get really ugly, if the other people watching the event—most of them Black—had decided to get involved.
>
> They didn't. Instead, they told the officer what he did was wrong and told him several times the entire incident had been caught on tape. (Abouhalkah, 2010, para. 6–7)

---

[1] A few respondents did uncloak the hypothesis that racial bias must have played a role in the incident, but these divergent entries tended to provoke rejoinders such as, "Not everything in life revolves around race" (Martinez, 2010, Comments section, p. 3), and "All this crap about race and teeny boppers really chaps my hind end" (Martinez, 2010, Comments section, p. 2).

STAGING A RECONCILIATION EVENT

The police–community relationship of today is obviously less polarized than that of the sixties, with an attenuation of inflexible positions, except among persons on the fringe. Illustrative of the new ethos is an event that took place in a Seattle high school 3 days after the videotaped incident. The event was spearheaded by James Kelly, the CEO of the Urban League, the individual who had initially remarked that the police ought to be ashamed of themselves. Mr. Kelly and his organization issued the following statement to announce the event they were sponsoring:

> Ms. Rosenthal and Officer Walsh have been in every major media report in the country since their Monday confrontation. At my request, the two met today just to see if we could calm down a growing volatile situation. This is the first step toward reconciliation and healing.
>
> This was not about cameras and charges and lawsuits and people getting into their own silos and protecting their own turf: This was about two human beings who might offer the rest of us a chance of learning from a situation which could present itself any time in any neighborhood with any one of us. ("Obama-Like Beer Summit," 2010, para. 4–5)

The Seattle Police Department issued a counterpart announcement under the signature of the interim chief:

> Officer Walsh was approached about this and agreed to meet with this young woman. He did not have to do this, but he felt it was an important step in the beginning of the healing process. I want to personally thank Officer Walsh for his willingness to participate in this dialogue in what has been, undoubtedly, a very stressful period.
>
> I would also like to thank Angel [Rosenthal]. I think her willingness to reach out to Officer Walsh shows bravery and maturity. We hope this meeting will take the focus off the video clip and place it where it belongs, the need for the renewed commitment to a conversation about race and social justice in this city. ("Obama-Like Beer Summit," 2010, para. 8–9)

The teenager, as instructed, apologized to the officer for her assertive intervention in the incident, including her intemperate remarks; the officer, as scheduled, accepted her apology. The teenager was accompanied at the meeting by her legal team. Notably absent was the King County prosecutor, who had indicated that he was charging the girl with assault.

POLICE–COMMUNITY RELATIONS, INSTITUTIONALIZED IN SEATTLE

The most literal reading of police–community relations suggests that there must be a payoff in forging person-to-person links between members of a police department and groups in the community. The most obvious perceived benefit would be a reduction in preexisting resentments and suspicion. The assumption would be that amiable encounters between citizens and police officers can neutralize the residues of less-than-amiable encounters. In this sense, the Urban League mediation session would be an exercise in police–community relations. The targets would not only be the two protagonists (though their meeting had a soap-operatic appeal) but also groups in the community whose antagonism to the police might have been reinforced by the jaywalking episode.

We have already noted that in the seventies, the police–community relations movement had relied on compartmentalized or delegated relationship building, mostly the work of officers attached to community-relations units and of newly hired paraprofessional linkage personnel. (There was also a great deal of talk about every police officer being in the community-relations business, but no one knew what this meant.) The early experiments may have been helpful as precursors to later developments, but most of the interventions were self-insulating and invited rejection within the police organization. Even attendance of police chiefs and commissioners at meetings of community groups could have adverse repercussions. They risked being discounted as ceremonial gestures among members of the community and as political posturing among officers.

Today, linkages between police and citizen groups have become by far the most prevalent tool of police reform (see Chapter 9, this volume). The

Seattle Police Department has been at the forefront of this trend and has taken advantage of every opportunity (and then some) to relate to one group or another in the community. The department created numerous advisory councils in the eighties, specialized community advisory councils in the nineties, and a city-wide advisory council in 2003. It has fielded teams to provide feedback at the precinct level and has an advisory body called Youth Outreach.

Today's department's website asserts the following:

> Community partnerships allow us to change the role of police from one of "rescuer" to that of "partner." We are especially proud of our innovative and successful community councils that
>
> > Allow individuals to participate based on where they live (geographic), who they are (demographic), or issue-related concerns. We also strive to work in concert with other city, county, and private businesses, as oftentimes, police action is only a small part of the solution to a problem. The Seattle Police Department welcomes community input, involvement, and feedback. We know that our ability to provide quality public services rests on the trust and support of those we serve. (http://www.seattle.gov/police/)

The department has stressed the importance of both formal and informal linking efforts, including social events. In a 2007 message, for example, the Seattle chief pointed out the following:

> The department has a variety of outreach efforts to allow the public and police employees to meet in more relaxed and fun environments. These programs include our Citizen Police Academy, our foundation-sponsored Picnic at the Precinct events, our Demographic Advisory Councils, Night Out Against Crime, and other prevention efforts. In 2007, in honor of the 50th anniversary of the musical *West Side Story*, our youth outreach officers partnered with the 5th Avenue Theater to introduce teens to the music and story and start a conversation about modern day gang issues and prevention. Programs such as these give the public and our employees opportunities to gain a better

understanding of each other and to share their unique perspectives. (Kerlikowske, 2007, p. 1)

"Gaining a better understanding of each other" is compatible with— but certainly not identical to—"changing the role of police to that of 'partner.'" There is nothing objectionable, of course, about overlapping objectives. Ambiguity of goals may be a public-relations asset rather than a liability where reform efforts are ongoing. However, we have to recognize that it is far easier to stage amiable encounters than to promote role changes, which invites resistance in the community and among the police. As Egon Bittner (1980) noted three decades ago, true police-community-relations reform presupposes that both ends can ultimately be attained. Bittner wrote:

> While civility and humaneness are desirable qualities in any person, and their possession may be indispensible for competent police work, they do not suffice. The opposite of the crude policeman is not one embued with civic virtues and possessed of a polite manner; instead, he is the informed, deliberating, and technically efficient professional who knows that he must operate with the limits set by a moral and legal trust. (p. 150)

A MULTITIERED EDIFICE FOR ENSURING TRANSPARENT ACCOUNTABILITY

The crisis that the police profession faced in the sixties left a lingering question as to the extent to which resentments in the ghetto about the perceived abuses of the police had dissipated or become attenuated over time. The recurrent evidence suggested that self-congratulations might not be in order. A study conducted by the Vera Foundation in Seattle thus confirmed what other surveys had suggested:

> Overall, [Seattle] citizens hold positive opinions of the police [and] among citizens who had recent contact with the police, satisfaction with officer performance was high. . . . [However,] a majority of city residents believe that racial profiling by police officers and stopping people without good reason are problems in Seattle. (Davis, Henderson, & Cheryachukin, 2004, p. i)

Among the most serious consequences was the following:

> Consistent with results from other surveys, the responses of Black residents were uniformly less positive than responses of members of other racial and ethnic groups. This difference was most apparent in opinions about police misconduct, where large majorities of Black residents believed that there were problems with the police stopping people without a good reason, engaging in racial profiling, and inflicting verbal or physical abuse upon citizens. (Davis, Henderson, & Cheryachukin, 2004, p. i)

The Seattle Police Department had gone to extraordinary lengths to attempt to address such concerns (Kerlikowske, 2001), and part of the department's response had been to create an internal investigation system with multiple safeguards. A key component of this system was the police auditor, a role that was introduced in Seattle in 1992. According to Samuel Walker (2005), "the police auditor is more likely to be an effective form of citizen oversight than a traditional civilian review board, and even more important, the police auditor has the potential for ensuring the long-term success of accountability efforts" (p. 135). Walker pointed out that

> the crucial aspect of the police auditor concept is its focus on organizational change. . . . Instead of focusing narrowly on the culpability of officers in particular misconduct incidents, police auditors focus on organizational problems that underlie such incidents. (p. 135)

The Seattle Police Department's internal review entity (called Office of Professional Accountability [OPA] to give it a touch of gravitas and a deployable set of initials) has a civilian director who reports to the chief. The OPA director is also a member of the chief's command staff, as is the director of community relations. The OPA has its own civilian review board, and the department has a community outreach manager. Moreover, as the auditor has noted, there is a great deal of decentralized community-relations activity in Seattle's diverse precincts, and "individual precincts have established their own various forms of community outreach, and the precinct captains set the tone for overall inclusiveness in the way [precinct] teams, coordinators and precinct councils . . . operate" (Pflaumer, 2009, p. 12).

THE PROFILING PROBLEM

The Seattle Police Department has issued a Policy and Procedures Bulletin (1.010) specifying the following:

> Race and or ethnicity shall not be motivating factors in making law enforcement decisions, and officers shall not (1) consider race or ethnicity in establishing either reasonable suspicion or probable cause; (2) consider race or ethnicity in deciding to initiate even those consensual encounters that do not amount to legal detention or to request consent to search. (Seattle Police Department, 2004)

In 2009, the department initiated a training program that is conducted by police officers, called "Perspectives in Profiling." One point that is covered in the training program, unfortunately, confirms that the profiling problem may be difficult to address:

> The training points out that there is a universal definition dilemma between law enforcement and members of the community about how to define racial profiling. Law enforcement tends to define racial profiling as action based solely on race—"stopping people because of race." Members of the community find reliance on race, whether in whole or in part, to constitute profiling—"use of race in traffic or pedestrian stops, even if race is only one of many factors used in a profile." (Pflaumer, 2009, pp. 7–8)

The principal difficulty—as in other settings where profiling has become an issue—has to do with statistics that show African Americans to be arrested or intercepted by the police in numbers disproportionate to their share of the population. The usual rejoinder—that the high percentages might be commensurate with violent-crime statistics—can make sense with regard to violent-crime arrests. However, the argument is not directly relevant when applied to nonviolent offenses such as jaywalking, and it becomes silly in defense of interceptions and searches in which no evidence of criminal involvement is uncovered (see Chapter 10, this volume). Fortunately, Seattle appears to be in the clear with regard to traffic stops, where "the racial numbers are roughly in proportion to the population figures for Seattle, consistent over three years reported: About 62% White, 17% African American, 9% Asian. These figures correlate closely with infractions documented by race" (Pflaumer, 2009, p. 5).

THE BYSTANDER PROBLEM

The Seattle Police Department recently issued a Policy and Procedures Bulletin (17.070) titled "Citizen Observation of Officers." The policy statement on the subject reads as follows:

> It is the policy of the Seattle Police Department that people not involved in an incident may be allowed to remain in proximity of any stop, detention or arrest, or any other incident occurring in public so long as their presence is lawful and their activities, including verbal comments, do not obstruct, hinder, delay, or threaten the safety or compromise the outcome of legitimate police actions and/or rescue efforts. Officers should assume that a member of the general public is observing, and possibly recording, their activities at all times. . . . With the prevalence of digital cameras, cell phones, cameras, etc. in existence, it is common for police incidents to be photographed by citizens as well as the media. . . . Officers shall recognize as well as obey the right of persons to observe, photograph, and/or make verbal comments in the presence of police officers performing their duties. (Seattle Police Department, 2008, p. 1)

This statement would have been utterly inconceivable (and difficult to accept) for officers in the sixties, who saw bystanders as trespassers on their turf who were uniformly alien and ill-intentioned. It would have been hard for the officers at the time to envision the notion that they "should assume that a member of the general public is observing, and possibly recording, their activities at all times" (Seattle Police Department, 2008, p. 1). In retrospect, however, that working assumption (if internalized) would have served as a deterrent to some outlandish uses of force.

Our West Coast City officers would have been more receptive to a provision of the Seattle Municipal Code (# 12.A.16.010) relating to the offense, "Obstructing a Public Officer." The offense (obstructing) is there defined as subsuming acts such as "intentionally and physically interferes with a public official," "intentionally hinders or delays a public officer by disobeying an order to stop given by such an officer," and "intentionally refuses to leave the scene of an investigation of a crime while an investigation is in progress after being requested to leave by a public officer" (cit. Pflaumer, 2008, p. 4).

In a carefully conducted study, the Seattle auditor posed questions (comparable to those we had broached in our West Coast City interviews) about officers who had accumulated a larger-than-usual number (three, four, or more) of arrests for obstruction only. In Seattle, no patterns or propensities of such officers were reportedly uncovered. Instead, the auditor found that

> the particular shift and beat of the arresting officers has a lot to do with the situations they repeatedly face of the street. The arrests tended to be concentrated in certain parts of town and notably on the nighttime watches. (Pflaumer, 2008, p. 8)

However, the auditor also noted that "there may be a significant increase in obstruction arrests where the officers are 'proactive,' as opposed to responsive to 911 calls" (Pflaumer, 2008, p. 8), which is the closest one may have come in Seattle to a behavior pattern or propensity.

With regard to the link of intervening bystanders to citizens, the auditor pointed out that "the bystander arrested for obstruction is often a friend or relative who wants to take control of a suspect and prevent his being taken into custody" (Pflaumer, 2008, p. 12), and she noted that "in approximately 19 cases, the defendants ran or walked quickly away from officers who [had] ordered them to stop" (Pflaumer, 2008, p. 10). This finding suggests that the jaywalking incident was in fact representative, as does the observation that "in about seven cases, the contact [with the bystanders] was for jaywalking or pedestrian interference" (Pflaumer, 2008, p. 7). The number is small, but the statistic helps to pose the challenging question asked by the auditor: "What are the legitimate costs of letting a jaywalker ignore an officer and keep walking versus insisting on going hands on when the jaywalker disrespects or disobeys the officer?" (Pflaumer, 2008, pp. 9–10).

THE POSSIBILITY OF DISENGAGEMENT

At one level, the auditor was asking something like, Can police officers legitimately disengage themselves from an escalating encounter that they might have unwittingly precipitated by responding to a minor transgression, if—should they persevere—they (and a group of citizens) would predictably become enmeshed in a messy confrontation? In the sixties, the answer to this question was unequivocally "no." The feeling at the time was that once an officer had initiated an intervention—no matter how silly or precipitous—he or she had to follow it through to the bitter end, because any disengagement would provide evidence of weakness and vulnerability, which would encourage perpetrators to perpetrate. This expectation implied an unflattering view of spectators to police incidents because it presupposed that they were incipient malefactors or were sufficiently in league with offenders to spread the news of any police vulnerability they had observed. This opinion was expressed not only with regard to officers' own interventions but also on behalf of the actions of other officers who might have been observed at the scene, no matter how stupidly or clumsily these officers might have behaved in initiating inappropriate confrontations.

The syllogism was also applied to the physical aspect of confrontations, which meant that if anyone grabbed, elbowed, pushed, or jostled an officer, a rejoinder would become inevitable because the nonescalation of force could be equated by spectators with fear-induced retreat. Members of the Seattle chorus appeared to endorse this perspective by repeatedly castigating the officer's opponent, in comments to news stories, on the ground that "one never lays hands on a cop" (Martinez, 2010). This was meant to convey not just that police are entitled not to have their uniforms wrinkled by pesky interlopers but also that—should such an incursion occur—any reasonable person would expect a ferocious response.

Curiously, no members of the chorus presumed that one could challenge the officer's decision to follow the girl who walked away from him and to detain her by grabbing her arm. Once an officer embarks on a potentially ill-fated initiative, the prevailing presumption is that it would be inconceivable (and unprofessional) for him or her not to follow through and to abandon the chase when his or her instructions have been ignored.

No blogger or commentator asked the question raised by the auditor: "Might an officer legitimately let a suspect walk off into the sunset in order to avoid a confrontation?" A contaminating factor in Seattle is that walking away from an officer is, by statute, a criminal offense. Another fact of life is that most officers resent passive–aggressive rejoinders to their instructions. As a rule, cops hate to be disrespected and ostentatiously ignored.

THE PERCEIVED LEGITIMACY OF INTERVENTIONS

At a more general level, the auditor raised questions about the priority assigned to jaywalking enforcement in Seattle. Based on her data relating to the volatility of these interventions, the auditor suggested that the strategy for addressing traffic safety concerns could stand a closer second look. The prospect of reexamining the jaywalking issue could find resonance with members of the chorus, including those who expressed support for the officer. The respondents argued that violence could be an understandable outcome when citizens see no reason for police intrusions into their lives and do not feel they have done anything to warrant being detained. The resentment in the incident at issue, however, was not most plausibly directed at the officer and his actions but at the source of the marching orders with which he was complying:

- Should the girl have punched the officer, no. Should the officer have punched the girl, we do not know. Should the officer be punished, no. (Martinez, 2010, Comments section, p. 1)
- But what is interesting is that all of this stemmed from a jaywalking incident. . . . I live in NYC and I jaywalk in front of the NYPD all the time and have never been stopped. I guess the NYPD has real criminals to catch, instead of jaywalkers like the Seattle PD. (Martinez, 2010, Comments section, p. 1)
- It is liberating leaving Seattle to visit some other U.S. cosmopolis . . . any place where the city council respects the intelligence of its citizens to cross against a red light or cross the middle of a street when no cars are present . . . Mr. Mayor, we've got brains here. Let us cross freely so we don't have to look so dorkish to out-of-towners who always look

perplexed when they see us standing at red lights when no cars are coming in either direction. ("Seattle Jaywalkers Unite," 2003, para. 1)

■ Go after murderers, thieves, and rapists. Leave the jaywalkers alone. (Bennett, 2010, Comments section)

Though the arguments are given in direct response to the incident, the resentments regarding jaywalking presumably are of long standing, because there is a history of public grousing on the subject. The Seattle Police Department would be cognizant of this fact. The following retrospect is from an article in *The Seattle Times:*

> Police say they ticket jaywalkers because a number of people in Seattle have been injured and killed dashing out into traffic in areas where drivers can't see them. Jaywalking near the site of Monday's incident . . . was cited as a major safety problem in the city's 2006 action plan. . . . The plan, which kicked off in April 2006, called for Seattle police to target jaywalkers there with added safety patrols. (Miletich, 2010, June 16, para. 10–12)

There is no indication that this reasoned rejoinder—including its supporting data—would put the argument to rest.

Police are on precarious ground when they intercept an individual to subserve some statistical probability. This is especially the case when police engage in preemptive enforcement—in interventions that the police contend are designed to prevent harm that has not yet occurred. It is not surprising that this justification is bound to ring hollow to its beneficiaries: Most of us experience ourselves as unique individuals. We do not see ourselves in statistical terms, and when we do, it is not likely to be in terms of whatever distribution the police have in mind. This disjuncture is important because it is where charges of profiling originate.

Today's penchant for preemptive enforcement in policing—particularly for "stop-and-frisk" incursions into large minority enclaves—has elevated the issue of police legitimacy in public discourse to a pitch we have not heard since the polarization of the sixties. Stop-and-frisk policing is, therefore, my concern in Chapter 10. Before that, I must revisit Seattle and its police department to accommodate some serious developments.

CODA

In December 2010, the police department announced that its Office of Professional Accountability had determined that the officer involved in the jaywalking incident had "acted within the scope of department policies and procedures" (Miletich, 2010, December 7a, para. 3). Some activists viewed this announcement as further documenting their allegation that the police department had engaged in a pattern of violating the civil rights of suspects, particularly minorities. The president of the Urban League issued a statement of his own, in which he asserted that "the department missed an opportunity . . . to increase its credibility, particularly in minority communities" (Miletich, 2010, December 7a, para. 5). Other responses were muted. Not only had the passage of time served to attenuate recollections of the original incident, but its aftermath also appeared calculated to modulate feelings. The two perpetrators were only nominally punished, earning terms of probation and community service. Neither of the girls had been jailed, and the jaywalking infraction was dismissed. The period had also produced police–citizen confrontations that overshadowed the jaywalking encounter. I turn to these developments in the next chapter.

8

A Posthumous Chorus and Street Justice in Seattle

On August 30, 2010, in downtown Seattle, an officer shot and killed a man who had refused to drop his knife when the officer ordered him to drop it. The man was a homeless alcoholic who had been seriously mentally ill. He also happened to be a Native American and a wood carver. The knife the man was carrying was stubby and had a 3-inch blade. The man had been using the knife to do his wood carvings, which he sold to a store that retailed them to tourists. He was also carrying a wooden board, which he had presumably intended to carve.

The shooting took place 12 days after the swearing in of Seattle's newly appointed police chief, who had indicated to the activists who made a point of attending his confirmation hearings that he would be attuned and responsive to the needs of the community. High on the roster of demands that the activists assertively presented was for the police to respond convincingly to allegations of profiling, to investigate uses of excessive force, and to show sensitivity to matters related to cultural diversity. The shooting of the wood carver reinvigorated the activists and helped make public many grievances of the Native–American community in Seattle that had previously been ignored.

THE MOBILIZATION OF THE CHORUS

The video of the wood carver incident—which was recorded by a camera in the officer's patrol car—was neither revealing nor available to the media. However, descriptive details were furnished to the press by the police and by witnesses, and the story percolated through both the traditional and nontraditional media. On the Internet, initial comments on the newspaper stories describing these reports almost uniformly questioned the judgment of the officer. Readers who deviated from the consensus ("I suppose permitting a drunk Japanese man to walk about swinging a samurai sword is likewise a requirement of cultural sensitivity?"; Madrid, 2010, Comments section) invited vigorous rejoinders ("Your analogy is a bad one"; Madrid, 2010, Comments section), including those from self-advertised police partisans ("I almost always side with the cops, and even I can see that this is a case of itchy trigger finger"; Madrid, 2010, Comments section).

The first convocation of the citizens as a collectivity took place two nights after the shooting and took the form of a candlelight vigil, with some 200 people in attendance. Participants in this event were described in newscasts as follows:

> Holding candles, praying, and singing for over two hours. . . . Members of [Indian] tribes in Alaska, Canada, many parts of Washington, and all plains nations were represented. City officials, most notably Mayor Mike McGinn and City Attorney Pete Holmes, stood in solidarity with the crowd. Elk stew and fry bread were served, as one by one people stood to eulogize Williams [the man who was shot] between songs and prayer. (Madrid, 2010, para. 1–2)

The newscasts also noted that "the peacefulness of the candlelight vigil couldn't mask the growing anger at the Seattle Police Department over Williams's death" (Madrid, 2010, para. 3) and that "outbursts of anger throughout the evening showed a lack of faith in the police—specifically, in police accountability—among the Native Americans and homeless people present" (Madrid, 2010, para. 8). One of the organizers of the vigil was quoted as telling the crowd, "This is a night of peace, love and prayer—not demonstration. But the demonstration is coming. We can't let something like this happen and not demand to see changes" (Madrid, 2010, para. 9).

The demonstration alluded to eventuated in due course. It was described as having been organized by a "range of civil-rights, faith, and community groups" (Mapes, 2010, para. 11). These organizers sent the mayor a formal announcement, containing "a list of demands, including appointment of a tribal liaison at the mayor's office" (Mapes, 2010, para. 11). The mayor responded by meeting with the demonstrators in the lobby of the city hall, where they congregated after marching in the rain through downtown Seattle:

> The demonstrators, many of them Native American or First Nations tribal members, carried branches of cedar, a symbol of cleansing and healing.
>
> They sang the songs of their ancestors all the way into City Hall, with its artwork representing Indian canoes, paddles, and cedar hats, evoking the city's roots.
>
> After a time of drumming, singing, and speeches, the mayor came to welcome the peaceful demonstration. "We all know the shooting of John Williams was a tragedy," McGinn said.
>
> He was surrounded by a group of singers and drummers, who offered a song intended to be medicine for his spirit. Handed a rolled-up T-shirt, he used it to pat his left palm in time with the drums. (Mapes, 2010, para. 3–6)

The events were covered on local television stations, and video clips that featured scenes from the march were circulated via blogs. Photographs of the march became available—in assorted sizes—via the Internet.

THE RESPONSE TO THE CHORUS

On September 15, 2010, the mayor and the chief of police held a news briefing to announce a series of impending changes in police management and operations,[1] with the mayor emphasizing that the reforms they were promulgating were not incident inspired but "reflective of concerns that

---

[1] Some of the changes were intended to emphasize the priority being accorded to community relations activities; others were routine reassignments of supervisory personnel by the newly appointed chief of police.

have been raised in the past" ("Hundreds Rally," 2010, para. 6). The mayor's caveat was not reflected the next morning in headlines such as "Activists Demand Change Within Police Department" (Haeck, 2010), "Officer's Shooting of Woodcarver Prompts Shake-up in Seattle Police Department" (Miletich & Heffter, 2010, September 15), and "Seattle Shakes up Police Command Ranks after Fatal Shooting of Woodcarver" (Miletich & Heffter, 2010, September 23). The theme carried through to accounts of the briefing, as in the following opening paragraphs:

> The sudden events that led Seattle police officer Ian Birk to fatally shoot a First Nations man on Aug. 30 lasted only a few moments.
>
> But reverberations from the confrontation prompted the Seattle Police Department on Wednesday to announce changes that could be felt for years.
>
> At a news briefing punctuated by pointed questions from community activists, Mayor Mike McGinn and Police Chief John Diaz laid out an ambitious plan to fundamentally alter the department's culture by requiring officers to deal more closely with the public and recognize different backgrounds. (Miletich & Heffter, 2010, September 15, para. 1–3)

Some of the reforms outlined at the press briefing involved higher echelon personnel shifts in the police department. The department, in a follow-up announcement, explained that the managerial reassignments were intended to ensure that "community building will be integrated at the highest staff levels into all day-to-day operations of the department to advance community policing principles" ("Seattle Police Chief," 2010, para. 3). The integrator-in-chief in the refurbished organization was a newly created "deputy chief of operations and community relations" [Chief Nick Metz], who was accorded "the responsibility of overseeing and coordinating all aspects of community outreach throughout the department, including Demographic Advisory Councils, Race and Social Justice Initiatives, and external communication" ("Seattle Police Chief," 2010, para. 4). "Operations" covers the bulk of police activities, so this meant that the person who was now overseeing community relations was concurrently responsible for day-by-day nuts-and-bolts policing. The linkage was intended to convey the message that "every employee of SPD will have responsibility in helping to build community" ("Seattle Police Chief," 2010, para. 4).[2]

TRAINING

A recurrent theme on the agenda of activists had been the reform of police training, on the assumption that abusive practices tend to result from neglectful indoctrination. In the wake of the wood carver incident, it was thus reported that "representatives of Native Americans and other minority groups and people from human- and civil-rights organizations demanded more training for police in everything from de-escalation to sign language" (Miletich & Heffter, 2010, September 15, para. 35). In less temperate terms, "the ACLU [American Civil Liberties Union] released a sharply worded letter . . . urging the department to change its attitude toward use of force and reevaluate its training" (Miletich & Heffter, 2010, September 23, para. 18). Although the police expressed reservations about the tone of the ACLU's letter, a deputy chief announced, "I want to say plainly that our training program is on trial right now," and the chief declared that "the department will conduct a systematic review of its training techniques . . . to be completed by Jan. 1" (Miletich & Heffter, 2010, September 15, para. 21–22). The chief did not specify who would be doing the reviewing nor whether he expected his systematic review to point to serious deficiencies in the department's training program, as was being implied by activist critics.

The training component that was seen to be most directly relevant to the wood carver incident was crisis intervention training, which deals with police responses to persons who are mentally ill or who demonstrate other disabilities. Whether such training had any bearing on the wood carver's shooting would of course have hinged on the officer being aware of the man's emotional and cognitive deficits. This consideration would also hold for other attributes of the wood carver that subsequently became

---

[2] To the uninitiated ear, this might appear to resemble the dictum "community relations is everybody's job," which was widely promulgated in the sixties but which had no tangible operational implications.

general knowledge, including the man's ethnicity, his partial deafness, and the fact that he was a carrying the tool of his trade. (Lack of awareness by the officer could of course be a reflection of defective powers of observation or failure to observe, and the officer might not have allowed himself the opportunity to ascertain facts that he ought to have ascertained.)

Another training component that was presumed by community activists to be relevant had to do with instruction relating to the decision to use lethal force. As a preemptive response to activists raising this issue, local reporters were taken on a guided tour of the training academy:

> [The staff] allowed the media to try out its "shoot or don't shoot" simulator that puts officers through different scenarios. Officers also go through tactics training in real-time mock situations. After the simulations, instructors debrief the officers to find out why they reacted the way they did. (Alder, 2010, para. 6)

But assuming the wood carver had indeed posed a threat (which at this stage was far from established), could less lethal responses have been available? Why had the officer not arrived at the scene equipped with a Taser and thoroughly trained in its use?

The Seattle Police Department announced that it had been planning to make Tasers more widely available to officers but questioned their applicability to the wood carver incident.[3] Deputy Chief Clark Kimerer explained to reporters that "officers are not trained to use the Taser against an armed person, unless they are accompanied by another officer who can provide, as he terms it, lethal cover" (Radil, 2010, September 24, para. 11). Academy instructors also pointed out that Tasers are often ineffective when the target happens to be intoxicated and/or mentally ill.

The type of training most frequently demanded by community activists was training designed to discourage racial profiling, though it is not obvious how such training would have applied to the wood carver incident. An in-service training module dealing with profiling had in fact been manda-

---

[3] The presumption relating to the deployment of less-than-lethal force is that it can substitute for the use of predictably lethal force. In practice, where Tasers (with their attendant risks) become readily available, they frequently come into use as an attractive alternative to verbal negotiation in conflict situations.

tory for Seattle police officers and civilian personnel (see Chapter 6, this volume). However, with respect to recruit training,

> Department officials also outlined their program to avoid racial profiling, which includes video simulation that required officer participation.
>
> In one scenario, an off-duty African-American officer is stopped by someone from her department who doesn't realize she is a cop. . . . The outcome of the video sequences can change during the scenario based on the reactions of officers. (McNerthney, 2010, September 22, para. 10–14)

ENSURING ACCOUNTABILITY AND TRANSPARENCY

The questions that were probably uppermost in the public's mind were whether the officer involved in the wood carver incident would be taken to account and whether the process that arrived at the judgment would be fair and dispassionate. To educate the media—and by extension, to reassure the chorus—the department provided a review of the initial phases of the process in an appendix to a news release. According to this review, the first step (already under way) would be an investigation of the wood carver's shooting by the homicide section of the department, which in this case needed to cover "the transcribed testimony of over 16 witnesses, extensive physical evidence—including video and audio recordings—and incident diagrams and scene recreations" (Office of the Mayor, 2010, p. 1). Once this investigation had run its course, the file would be submitted for preliminary review and supplementation. Within the department, the file would be transmitted to members of the Firearms Review Board (FRB), a body whose job it would be to decide whether the shooting might be justifiable. Externally, the information would be shared with the county prosecutor.

In the case of the wood carver incident, an additional reviewing body was to be introduced at this point to provide added reassurance to the public:

> The department is prepared to submit the complete and unedited investigation to two comparable police agencies to undertake a peer review. The criteria for the request to these peer agencies is that they

are comparable in size or larger than the Seattle Police Department and recognized on a national level for their major crime investigation thoroughness and credibility. The scope of this review will be to examine every facet of the department's investigation and determine if there are any gaps, omissions, inconsistencies, or investigative requirements that were unmet. (Office of the Mayor, 2010, p. 1)

This unprecedented step appeared intended to provide reassurance to persons who might not be ready to believe that a police department could dispassionately investigate one of its members.

CIVILIAN PARTICIPATION IN THE FIREARMS REVIEW BOARD

In accord with official Seattle Police Department policies and procedures (Section 1.305), an FRB is convened under the following circumstance:

Whenever there is an intentional discharge of a firearm by an officer and after each accidental discharge resulting in injury or death . . . to investigate and review the circumstances of that discharge, making findings and recommendations to the chief of police . . . who makes a determination whether or not the shooting was justified. (Seattle Police Department, 2010)

Among the questions an FRB would be required to answer is whether an officer had "probable cause to believe that the suspect . . . posed a threat of physical harm to the officer or . . . to others" (Seattle Police Department, 2010, Section 1.305) The FRB would also be asked to determine whether some action of the officer might have provoked the behavior that ended up posing the threat. This would be the case if an officer had forcibly restrained someone, caused the person to react in a panic, and then responded by shooting him or her.

The FRB comprises four higher echelon members of the police department and two observers. One observer is the representative of the police officers' union (the Seattle Police Officers Guild). The other is a civilian appointed by the mayor. The two observers participate in the FRB's inquiry, but they are not involved in the final deliberations. The civilian observer, however, had recently indicated that being excluded from the deliberation phase of the meetings had made her "feel ineffective" (Radil, 2010, September 17, para. 7). The city council convened a committee meeting in response, and one of its members pointed out with the hint of a threat that "the public would also want a citizen to be present during deliberations" (Bhattacharjee, 2010, para. 5). The guild president said that he did not share the civilian observer's frustrations but added that his organization was open to negotiating changes that could respond to her concerns (Heffter, 2010). The chief and the mayor indicated that they would favorably consider expanding the civilian observer's role on the FRB.

FRBs are internal review bodies in police departments, and they are defined as such because FRB recommendations involve professional judgments and contribute to the assessment of individual officer performance. It was therefore an extraordinary move for Seattle to include a civilian observer on the board. This the city council did in 2006 "to increase the confidence of the general public in the review process" (Seattle City Council, 2006, para. 4). The city council defined the observer's role as including contributing to reform. It thus required the observer to "meet periodically with the mayor, city council, and the police chief regarding recommendations to improve the firearms review process within the framework of applicable law and labor agreements" (Seattle City Council, 2006, para. 3).[4]

THE FIREARMS REVIEW BOARD FINDING

On October 13, 2010, it was reported that the FRB and chief of police had agreed on the preliminary finding that the shooting of the wood carver on August 30, 2010, was not justified (McNerthney & Gutierrez, 2010). The additional information that became available was that the officer involved in the incident had been placed on administrative leave and been ordered

---

[4]The city council did not make the observer's position a remunerative one. His or her compensation was fixed at "$150 for each hearing of the FRB" (Seattle City Council, 2006, para. 5), with no mention of cost-of-living increases.

to surrender his gun and badge. The next scheduled step in the process was the convening of an inquest, to be ordered by the county executive (the county containing Seattle does not have a coroner). Such a move is required by statute for "any death involving a member involving a law enforcement agency . . . while in the performance of his/her duties."

The FRB's finding elicited approval among members of the public, but the prevailing view was that the officer would probably be exonerated by the inquest jury and by the courts if he were prosecuted. One blog headline read, "John T. Williams Inquest: Don't be Surprised if His Death was Found Justified" (Anderson, 2010), and it elicited comments such as, "The inquest hearings are structured to give [police officers] a pass any time they claim their lives are in danger. And of course that's all the time" (Anderson, 2010, Comments section) and "[The officer] may lose his job, but that's all. That's how the system has always worked. I was part of it" (Anderson, 2010, Comments section). In a related story, the guild president was quoted as pointing out that "no officer has been charged with a crime over use of force since the early 1970s" (Miletich & Sullivan, 2010, October 14, para. 14).

An inquest in Seattle involves a judge, an eight-person jury, and two attorneys who cross-examine witnesses. The process may look like a trial but is carefully defined as a "public inquiry." It is an intervening step in a sequence of steps. The testimony at the inquest can help the prosecutor to decide whether he wants to charge an officer with a crime. The disposition assists a police department in arriving at a determination of its punitive disposition. Despite such interconnections, the decisions inside and outside the department are presumed to be independent of each other. This inspired one blog to observe, "Maybe the inquest jury is flying in from Mars where they have a news blackout, huh?" (Workman, 2010, para. 3).

ANOTHER DAY, ANOTHER VIDEOTAPE

During the period before the wood carver inquest was scheduled, a television station (KIRO) aired a new tape that featured an undercover officer in the apparent act of stomping a Black youth in a convenience store. A second television station (KOMO) aired another tape that was said to show the same officer assaulting a citizen in front of the store to discourage the citizen from memorializing the first incident with his cell phone.

When the Seattle chief was asked about the tapes, his concern was exacerbated by the revelation that the first video (recorded by a convenience store surveillance camera) had been in the department's possession all along, although its questionable content had not been shared with the chain of command. A deputy chief announced that "that is a concern and it is a focal point of the internal investigation" ("Video Appears to Show," 2010, para. 11).

The incident in the store had been an outgrowth of an earlier encounter—a drug-buy operation that had degenerated into a robbery attempt by the perpetrators in which two officers had been injured. The youth in the store was said to be a member of the group that had injured the officers, and his assailant had been one of their colleagues. The source of the officer's resentment therefore appeared to be obvious, which may have accounted for the fact that his behavior had initially not rung any alarm bells. The department's leadership, however, was less forgiving than the detectives who had reviewed the tape. A deputy chief emphasized that "our officers cannot afford to give in to emotion, and I think we give a very clear statement about that every time we can" ("Video Appears to Show," 2010, para. 9). He also indicated that the officer featured on the tape had been sent home "on administrative leave" ("Seattle Police Look," 2010, para. 3).

Citizen opinion of the department's response was divided. The question that was of most concern to the chorus was how much weight to assign to the righteousness of the officer's indignation. Would the young man's involvement in a police assault mitigate the officer's transgression?

> It does make a difference in my mind if the officer who'd done the kicking had just been beaten by this guy.

> He was beaten by these thugs. I can understand that affecting his judgment.

> If any officer reacts emotionally (like this guy) then he shouldn't be an officer.

> Emotions aren't controlled with a switch. . . . If you are old enough to be dealing drugs and planning beatings . . . then suffer the results of getting caught.

Chasing down the thug who initially assaults you is NOT self-defense but rather revenge, which is what this officer was engaged in.

He should be criminally charged with assault. ("Seattle Police Look," 2010, Comments section)

A few respondents drew distinctions between some of the officer's actions and others (such as the third kick, which appeared to have been aimed at the head). This critique elicited a response from the president of the police guild, who said, "It's getting kind of old to hear these Monday morning quarterbacks coming in and telling officers from a snippet of video how to do their job or what they should or shouldn't have done" (Byron, 2010, para. 3). In any event, according to the guild president, "The officer didn't kick the teen in the groin or in the head but only near these locations . . . two techniques taught in undercover training" ("Seattle Police Union," 2010, para. 8). He further described the officer's actions as efforts to secure compliance from a resistant arrestee:

What you don't see [in the video] is that outside the store, the officer had been telling him to get on the ground. He gave him half a dozen verbal demands to get on the ground. And he thought it would be okay to flee the officer, ignore the commands, and run into the store. ("Seattle Police Union," 2010, para. 7)

As expected, several community activists raised the issue of racial discrimination, with the guild president responding, "I don't care what color they are; a criminal is a criminal" (Miletich & Sullivan, 2010, November 18, para. 18). This view was elegantly phrased but was not shared by the director of the Washington ACLU, who insisted that the police department had been demonstrating a propensity to engage in civil rights violations:

[She said] the ACLU will send a request letter next week to the U.S. Justice Department, along with documentation of the incidents. "These repeated incidents over the past 18 months which have continued without forceful intervention by the Seattle Police Department, the mayor, or Seattle's other elected officials, leads the ACLU to call on the U.S. Department of Justice to investigate whether there is a pattern and practice of civil-rights violations by the Seattle Police

> Department in violation of the Constitution and federal law," the
> organization said in a written statement. (Miletich & Sullivan, 2010,
> November 18, para. 2–3)

The allegation that there had been no "forceful intervention" by the city or department leadership would be difficult to square with widely known facts, such as the repeated supplementation of multitiered reviewing procedures with additional ad hoc steps, such as interagency peer reviews. The rest of the ACLU's charges helped raise interesting questions about (a) the extent to which incidents of police misconduct can add up to a "pattern" (instead of being a cluster of unrelated events), (b) the extent to which the involvements of individual officers can be attributed to a "culture" that reinforces transgressions, and (c) the extent to which leaders of an organization such as a police department can shape the views and behavior of its rank and file.

Most members of the chorus in Seattle had no difficulty discriminating among individual officers and individual incidents. In their comments in response to the many news reports, the jaywalking encounter (see Chapter 6, this volume) was characterized as the lamentable result of an overtaxed officer's understandable frustration (resulting mostly from having to deal with two obstreperous young ladies simultaneously), whereas kicking the young suspect (the kung fu display) in the convenience store was seen as an out-of-control expression of retaliatory rage. Chorus members adjudged the killing of the wood carver to have been a tragic mistake, an officer's inappropriate appraisal of what citizens felt was a nonexistent threat. In each case, the public's understanding and evaluation of an encounter were appropriately informed by factual details revealed in video clips and reinforced by thoughtful discussion.

CAN THE CHIEF SHAPE THE LOCKER ROOM?

The issue of police leadership was brought to the fore by the perceived withholding of the kung fu officer tape. The tape had been viewed by Seattle detectives and retained in their files as documentation of the arrest effectuated in the convenience store. The detectives who had viewed the tape had not alerted anyone in the organization to the circumstances of the arrest. In assessing the situation as not being newsworthy, they had probably considered that the perpetrator had been involved in an assault on officers who had been injured. They may also have noted that the abusive behavior had been short circuited at its inception, with a second officer holding back the first to prevent him from proceeding.

High-ranking officers in the department made fewer accommodations as they viewed the arrest depicted in the tape. They may have been influenced by the fact that the scenario had become public knowledge, but they would unquestionably have been shocked under any circumstances. And as leaders of an organization that places considerable stress on community relations, they had evidence that seemed to show that other members of the organization had made inappropriate allowances in viewing the same shocking scenario. It might have appeared to them that the mission of the organization had not been understood and internalized.

Police officers, in Seattle and elsewhere, are not indifferent to the flagrant misbehavior of other officers. With respect to the convenience store scenario, a police blog elicited comments such as the following:

> The third kick, to the head, I don't know what he's gonna say about that.
>
> The uniformed (bike) cop [who is shown in the video restraining the first officer] deserves BIG credit for quelling what could have been a more precarious situation.
>
> I'm not going to judge the officer on what I can see in the video. That doesn't mean someone else isn't going to, obviously.
>
> I hope he can explain it and it is justified. But that will depend on facts NOT visible in the video. ("Seattle PD Investigates," 2010, Member Comments section)

Police officers tend to have a keen eye for detail and a sense of how the public (and the police leadership) is apt to respond to any given scenario. If they observe an instance of flagrant misbehavior, they are in a position that is comparable to surgeons in a hospital watching a colleague sewing up a patient after leaving his forceps in the man's chest. However, for surgeons to recognize malpractice does not mean that they favor malpractice litigation. Differences of views often have to do with what to do with the facts, such as whether an officer's misbehavior should be publicized and how it should be punished. Disagreements can also occur in situations that are less than clear cut, where facts are in dispute, or where they remain to be clarified. Such divergences of perspective are both understandable and predictable between ranks, given the leadership's responsibility to the community and the officers' empathetic resonance to each other. However, distances are easier to bridge once the facts are laid out and there can be agreement about the seriousness of the violation. For this reason, a dispassionate internal affairs process is important, inside as well as outside the police department.

OUTSOURCING THE KUNG FU INVESTIGATION

As soon as the convenience store incident was brought to the attention of the chief, he ordered that it be subjected to an "expedited review." At the time, a deputy chief explained to the press that "one issue under examination is why lower-ranking officers didn't report the video's content to the department's Office of Professional Accountability or through the chain of command" (Miletich, 2010, November 23, para. 17). The deputy chief added, "The state patrol might be better suited to look into that matter" (Miletich, 2010, November 23, para. 17). The police guild president indicated that the union "wouldn't object to an outside agency 'shadowing' Seattle police to ensure the incident was properly investigated" but would take exception to the investigation being taken over (Miletich, 2010, November 23, para. 20).

Thereafter, top-level negotiations took place between two agencies and resolved that the state police would undertake a criminal investigation of the incident while the Seattle department's internal affairs inquiry was put on hold. A Seattle union spokesperson snidely suggested that the state patrol was "not known for their expertise in these matters" (Miletich, 2010, December 7b, para. 15). This drew a huffy rejoinder from the state police, to the effect that "the agency's criminal division has considerable experience conducting investigations into the use of force by law-enforcement officers" (Miletich, 2010, December 7b, para. 17).

Interestingly, the story about the investigation of the incident appeared to revitalize the chorus that had been agonizing about the officer's culpability. New details were now introduced in comments on the news story on the basis of renewed scrutiny of the tape by members of the chorus and on the basis of rumors that had been circulating (Miletich, 2010, December 7b). Several commentators now asserted that the young man in the store could not have participated in the mugging because the tape showed that he had entered from a different direction. There was also a mini-debate among commentators about racism, which was prompted by someone's assertion, "I have taken several racial-sensitivity classes [and] usually, racism is not involved in incidents involving two people of color" (Miletich, 2010, December 7b, Comments section).[5] Finally, there was an extended and spirited discussion about the controversial third kick:

> The whole body language of the cop says "frustration," so he lashes out with his foot.
>
> Looks to me like the suspect grabs the officer's foot to prevent getting kicked in the head AGAIN.
>
> It looks like the officer slipped and his foot went out from under him.
>
> [*Response:*] You're joking, right? (Miletich, 2010, December 7b, Comments section)

Not one member of the chorus mentioned that he or she felt reassured by the fact that the investigation had been turned over to the state police, and many of the respondents voiced reservations about police investigations in general, irrespective of jurisdiction and affiliation.[6]

---

[5] Research by a member of the chorus had revealed that the family of the officer involved in the incident had originated in the Pacific islands.

[6] In this connection, it is important to keep in mind that the degree to which the views of the chorus may be representative of public opinion may vary from issue to issue, or among situations. The chorus is thus likely to be more cynical than the general public.

SPINNING THE WOOD CARVER INQUEST

Once a January inquest to look into the wood carver shooting had been scheduled, the presumption was that the contending parties would refrain from circulating information that could prejudice the jury. This understanding was mostly honored through its breach. The prosecutor's office eventually responded to public disclosure requests by releasing videos featuring prior contacts between the wood carver and the police. On most videos, the wood carver appeared to be intoxicated and uncooperative. On occasions his behavior bordered on the belligerent, though he usually complied with officers who treated him with consummate diplomacy. One of the viewers noted the following:

> The thing I take away from this story is how amazing most cops are in dealing with the regulars on their beat. The regular cops knew Williams and treated him the way you'd want cops to deal with a basically harmless guy. It's a shame that Williams ran into one who clearly didn't have the background and didn't know the beat he was patrolling. (Carter & Miletich, 2010, Comments section)

If a concerned party had hoped the release of the videos that documented the wood carver's past contacts with police officers might prejudice the public against the wood carver, they were mistaken. Respondents to the tapes not only restated the view that the wood carver was an innocent victim but also expressed resentment against what they perceived to be efforts to manipulate the public. These efforts they mostly blamed on the police:

> This is just media hype and damage control by the police department . . . [it] has absolutely nothing to do with the way this officer snuffed him out like a candle without probable cause to even stop him.
>
> He was belligerent in the past? Sounds like grounds for shooting him in cold blood.
>
> Yeah. I'm drunk. I'm belligerent. Shoot me. After all, you have a gun and I don't.
>
> Not that the SPD is trying to influence anything here—cough. Save this stuff for the courtroom. (Carter & Miletich, 2010, Comments section)

An even stronger response arose several days later after a judge ordered the release of the tape from the officer's dashboard camera, over the objection of his attorney. This video drew an avalanche of comments, almost all of which characterized the situation (especially as it unfolded in the timed audio portion of the video) as a scenario of cold-blooded murder.[7]

> [The officer] says drop the knife, and 4 seconds later he is shooting— Williams had no chance. The whole thing is shocking.

> He never gave the man a chance. Even a marine in Afghanistan, faced with a real enemy, would have the courage to assess the situation before opening fire.

> It happened so fast. I don't see how anyone would have time to turn around and figure out what was going on before he opened fire.

> I just watched this—twice—to confirm what I saw the first time. This was an assassination. (Miletich, 2010, December 17)

THE INQUEST AND THE CHORUS

The formal inquiry into the death of John Williams at the hands of Officer Ian Birk of the Seattle Police Department convened on January 10, 2011. The trial-like proceeding concluded 10 days later with the publication of individual responses by the eight inquest jurors to 13 questions posed to them by the presiding judge.

The inquest process provided continuing grist for the mills of concerned spectators through a generous supply of new and familiar details, and offered direct experiential access to this information on an ongoing basis. Video- and audiotapes of testimony were almost instantaneously available on every local source, as were videos of the scenario leading up to the incident and its aftermath. *The Seattle Times* reliably provided daily front-page coverage. It also offered a forum for comments from readers.

This *Seattle Times* forum became the vehicle for the chorus to voice its views. The responses primarily revolved around strongly felt concerns

---

[7] One respondent tentatively suggested that he might not have wanted to encounter Williams (the wood carver) in a dark alley. He was smothered with rejoinders that contended that the real risk would be to run into the officer who killed Williams.

about the perceived disproportionality of the officer's use of force (for the historical precedent, see Chapter 3, this volume), but feelings about injustice and discrimination were also voiced and generalized to the police department and the criminal justice system. Of course, the inquest was not set up to offer closure or resolution, and predictions about the outcome of the process were not satisfying to most spectators.

On January 9, 2011, the paper's headline emphasized that the inquest would "leave tough decisions for others" (Miletich, 2011, January 9). The story also pointed out that "inquest juries generally have found that officers have acted properly" (Miletich, 2011, January 9, para. 4) and mentioned that "state law makes it extremely difficult to bring criminal charges against a police officer who uses deadly force" (Miletich, 2011, January 9, para. 5). The story concluded that "in essence, if a police officer believes he was justified in using deadly force, prosecutors must overcome a steep hurdle to obtain a conviction" (Miletich, 2011, January 9, para. 28). According to the same story, the Seattle Police Guild might have opposed "any discipline" (Miletich, 2011, January 9, para. 44). This latter point prompted a reader to complain, "There is no end to what 'good' cops will do to protect 'bad' cops" (Miletich, 2011, January 9, Comments section).

The chorus reacted to each daily account but reached its crescendo in response to stories relating to the cross-examination of the officer (485 comments in total) and the testimony of witnesses who contradicted the officer's version of the shooting (549 and 433 comments, respectively, in total).[8] The officer's version of events met with almost universal disapproval, as did the testimony of a detective who contended that he had followed training guidelines. This initial day of the inquest elicited comments such as the following:

> Can't have some half deaf guy with a limp taking more than seconds to do whatever a voice yells at him!

> The idea that in 15 seconds Williams transformed from shuffling slowly across the street to some kind of ninja warrior is preposterous.

---

[8] Nationwide choruses can put such local responses to shame. An article in *Time* magazine about a controversial book on child rearing thus reported that "a prepublication excerpt in the *Wall Street Journal* . . . started a ferocious buzz; the online version has been read more than one million times and attracted *more than 7,000 comments* [emphasis added] so far" (Paul, 2011, p. 36).

"Hey, hey put the knife down!" Then BANG BANG BANG BANG BANG! Some training!

And by the way, the Nazis operating the ovens were just "following training" as well. (Miletich & Clarridge, 2011, Comments section)

Some commentators cautioned that all information was not yet in, but such reservations dissipated following the cross-examination and the testimony of witnesses who did not concur with the officer's account. With respect to his explanation of his actions, special attention was reserved for the assertion that he needed to shoot because the wood carver had "displayed 'pre-attack indicators' that included a clenched jaw, furrowed brows, and a fixed 'thousand-yard stare'" (Miletich & Clarridge, 2011, para. 13). One of the respondents proclaimed in reply, "Attention, Seattle visitors: A set jaw and a stern look can get you killed by the police" (Miletich & Clarridge, 2011, Comments section). Another respondent wrote, "This morning I spent a little time in front of the bathroom mirror making sure I didn't have a furrowed brow or a thousand-yard stare. I think I'm OK, but it's tough to say for sure" (Miletich & Clarridge, 2011, Comments section).

A minority of respondents objected to the univocal condemnation of the police. These dissenters presented a delicate problem to the rest of the chorus. On the one hand, the feeling was that police apologists were expressing offensive and implausible opinions. On the other hand, it is an article of faith among choristers that the opportunity to voice one's opinions is a prized vehicle for social reform. The dissonance in this instance was resolved by means of mini-dialogues allowing for contemptuous rejoinders:

As long as you don't walk around brandishing a weapon, you will be all right.

[*Response:*] I saw the video just like you did. Nobody was "brandishing a weapon." Nobody except the out of control rogue cop, that is. And being drunk is not a capital offense.

Apparently everyone has convicted Birk in the court of public opinion.

[*Response:*] Yes, we have convicted Birk in the court of public opinion. But we have done so after reviewing the totality of the evidence presented to us.

It is also not all right to lynch Birk based on his lack of police skill.

[*Response:*] Far better we are angry people here at our computers than circling the court house with pitchforks and torches. But then, I guess what some of the most angry on here have said about Williams *isn't* lynching?

[*And what may be the ultimate all-purpose rejoinder:*] You're just repeating talking points you heard down at the cop house, aren't you?

THE INQUEST JURY'S AMBIVALENT RESPONSE

On the morning of January 19, 2011, *The Seattle Times* listed 13 questions that had been posed to the inquest jury, while reminding its readers that "the inquest is not a trial, but an inquiry into circumstances and causes of the shooting" (Sullivan, 2011, para. 13). The questions were therefore of a strictly factual nature, designed to reconstruct the course of events leading to the shooting of the wood carver. The circumscribed inquiry predictably did not satisfy respondents who wanted culpability unambiguously assigned to the officer. Several commentators complained about what they saw as "powder-puff questions" (Sullivan, 2011, Comments section). Another wrote that "I must point out the obvious: This inquest 'trial' will never be confused with 'Judgment at Nuremberg'" (Sullivan, 2011, Comments section).

As it happens, the inquiry was not as tame as these comments implied. A January 20, 2011, article thus reported that half of the inquest jurors felt Williams had not had time to drop the knife (Miletich, & Sullivan, 2011, January 20). The story also pointed out that when jurors were asked whether, "based on the information available at the time," the wood carver "pose[d] an imminent physical threat of serious physical harm to Officer Birk" only one juror said yes, but four said no. On the other side of the ledger, four jurors were reported feeling that the officer thought the wood carver was a threat when he fired his weapon (Miletich & Sullivan, 2011, January 20). The fact that this verdict was a mixed bag was illustrated by the reactions of the two opposing lawyers, each of whom declared himself vindicated by one or another set of responses (Miletich & Sullivan, 2011). Last, *The Seattle Times* published an editorial on January 21, 2011, that argued that "this troubling case needs . . . to move ahead with some final-ity" ("The Williams Case," 2011, para. 2). The editorial's prescription, ironically, represented a compromise, in that the editors concluded, "The shooting death of John T. Williams might not be criminal, but it also might not be tolerable for those who work to protect the community" ("The Williams Case," 2011, para. 12). This sentence contained a broad hint that would likely not be overlooked by the Seattle Police Department, its shooting review board, and its leadership.

9

Learning to Live
With Due Process

The events in Seattle that I have been describing culminated in February 2011—or at least reached a point that offered a measure of closure to members of the Seattle chorus, who had been calling for retributive justice and radical (but unspecified) reforms of the police. In the wake of the inquest (see Chapter 8, this volume), the mayor and police chief preemptively organized an open public forum at city hall. This encounter was described by the press as "heated" and as unfolding "amid catcalls and angry outbursts" (Miletich, 2011, February 3, para. 1, 2). The mayor and the chief, however, persevered under fire and communicated to the audience their resolve to move as expeditiously as possible to initiate responsive interventions.

At some point during the session, the president of the police union took the stage and offered his organization's support for reform. He was quoted as having said, "Mr. Mayor, I'm here to tell you the union is a partner in the system," and he mentioned as evidence that "the guild has twice agreed in the last 10 years to major reforms in internal investigations and discipline" (Miletich, 2011, February 3, para. 18). Unfortunately, the president was also goaded into making a short unscheduled comment in response to a question from the floor:

> The discussion among panelists was marked by blunt exchanges, including one in which Sgt. Rich O'Neill, president of the Seattle Police Officers' Guild, told the audience that incidents wouldn't happen if citizens complied with the orders of police, *even if the officers were wrong* [emphasis added]. (Miletich, 2011, February 3, para. 11)

O'Neill's rejoinder proved to be less than felicitous in the context of prevalent resentments, such as those revived by the inquest. The reply drew readers' comments such as the following:

> The most prominent enabler and encourager of police misconduct and murder seems to be the union president.
>
> The concept that police are entitled to abuse their authority the moment someone doesn't comply to their satisfaction, is outrageous.
>
> The opportunity to slap my wife around wouldn't exist as much if she just did what I told her—even when I'm wrong.
>
> Rich O'Neill is an anachronism. (Miletich, 2011, February 3, Comments section)

The union president's unscheduled response also drew an editorial rebuke from *The Seattle Times* ("Seattle Police Officers," 2011). The editors opined, "A pattern of excessive force by police, including the shooting death of a native woodcarver, took O'Neill's remark from arrogant to frightening" ("Seattle Police Officers," 2011, para. 3).

Concurrently, a series of responses to the forum story began to appear in defense of O'Neill and his beleaguered colleagues. The respondents expressed the view that law enforcement is a difficult and thankless endeavor, especially in a city like Seattle, where the respondents felt that disrespect for authority was widely nurtured, admired, and reinforced:

> Personally, I think you would have to be partially insane to want to be a cop in today's freakish society.

Disrespect for authority appears to be the norm.

One reason for so many problems in Seattle is because we promote contempt for authority.

I bet most of you wouldn't make it past the "You honky pig!" comment before you begin roughing up the scum calling you names. (Miletich, 2011, February 3, Comments section)

One of the most prolific members of the Seattle chorus (credited with over 2,300 entries) was keeping an eye on the comments as they appeared and hypothesized that the dissenting views were the product of a campaign that had been initiated by the police union. He wrote:

The comments ratings got so switched around in the last 12 hours, from mostly negative towards police brutality to being pro police brutality while also trying to deflect blame on Williams' family for not helping him, shows the effectiveness of the e-mail campaign from the Seattle Police Officers Guild directing officers to log in and comment and rate posts. (Miletich, 2011, February 3, Comments section)

This assertion might or might not have been accurate, but it is unquestionable that collective expressions of opinion vary in the extent to which they are spontaneous. Internet comments are not concurrent independent entries expressing individual views. At minimum, participants in the blogosphere become aware of other participants and cognizant of the positions they have recorded. To varying degrees, susceptible individuals can be influenced by the views of fellow choristers, and collusions (or competing collusions) can take place.

Comments can be reinforced, but they can also be drowned out. Lost in the heat of the dialogue following the public meeting, for example, was the recollection of a member of the audience who alleged that O'Neill's intervention at the session was unfairly highlighted in newspaper accounts: "I was there last night. O'Neill also said, 'Anytime there is a perception, regardless of whether it's based on reality or not, we need to address it.'" (Miletich, 2011, February 3, Comments section).

EXIT THE DESIGNATED VILLAIN, STAGE LEFT

At the inception of the wood carver incident, the Seattle mayor and police chief felt obligated to reiterate that due process had to be observed. However, both the mayor and the chief were aware of the anger the incident had generated, which was directed not only at the officer but also at the department in which he was now nominally employed. The mayor and chief were also aware of the impatience of the chorus at the conclusion of the inquest. They therefore emphasized that decisive actions would be taken as quickly as possible and that each move along the way would be publicly accessible and transparent.

Within days of the promulgated resolve, a succession of developments brought the wood carver story to an unexpected climax. Three publicized events occurred in close succession on Wednesday, February 16, 2011. The day opened with a press conference by the county prosecutor, who reported that after close inquiry he had been forced to the reluctant conclusion that it would be futile to charge the officer, given provisions in state statutes that called for evidence of malicious intent. This announcement was followed later in the day by a news release from the office of the chief of police. In this release, the police department confirmed that the Firearms Review Board had adjudged the shooting of the wood carver to be unjustifiable. This verdict came buttressed with a book-length report that documented both the process and the findings the board had arrived at, many of which some members of the chorus had anticipated. In releasing the report, the chairman of the board said, "These are among the most egregious failings I have seen" (Miletich & Sullivan, 2011, February 16, para. 37). He also said that "it was heart-wrenching, because what we were seeing was an outcome that could have been avoided" (Miletich & Sullivan, 2011, February 16, para. 38).

The third of the developments was a statement from the chief of police, which read as follows:

> Officer Ian Birk has communicated to me his intent to resign his commission with the Seattle Police Department.
> His resignation will take place effectively at 4 p.m. today.

At my direction, the Office of Professional Accountability investigation will continue forward. The completion of this investigation is not contingent on Ian Birk remaining on the force. Reaching our administrative conclusion is a necessary step to providing a small degree of closure to the many people affected by this tragedy over the past several months. (Seattle Police Department, 2011, para. 1–3)

The mayor's office issued its own statement, which reiterated that proprieties had to be observed but that it was "clear that Officer Birk saw the writing on the wall. He could read the same Firearms Review Board report that the rest of us did" (McGinn, 2011, para. 2). The mayor's office emphasized that "the final OPA [Office of Professional Accountability] review will continue, so that the department can properly close the case and recommend to the state whether Birk should be allowed to work elsewhere as a police officer" (McGinn, 2011, para. 3).

DIVERGENT PERSPECTIVES

News accounts at the end of the day stressed the interconnectedness of events. The opening sentence of one article read, "Seattle police officer Ian Birk bowed Wednesday to what appeared to be his certain firing, resigning hours after department brass released a scathing report of his fatal shooting of wood carver John T. Williams" (Miletich & Sullivan, 2011, February 16, para. 1). The news story hinted at a lack of resolution in the minds of the chorus. It noted that "Birk's departure resolved one issue in the city's most controversial police shooting in years, but not the widespread anger and distrust that it has generated" (Miletich & Sullivan, 2011, February 16, para. 6).

The story also quoted the prosecutor—who had himself just become the source of "widespread anger and distrust"—to the effect that "the reaction to the shooting has sparked a 'deep divide' in the community as well as in the police department" (Miletich & Sullivan, 2011, February 16, para. 19). The mayor added:

I know the public finds the lack of action frustrating. . . . So do I. The laws that govern this issue place greater value on the officer's due process rights, and rights in his job, than the public's expectation that improper use of force will be swiftly and appropriately dealt with. (Miletich & Sullivan, 2011, February 16, para. 26)

The union president, however, was not in a position to abandon "the officer's due process rights" that the mayor was alluding to. He said that in meetings with the officer and guild attorney, options had been discussed that included "appeal rights and the possibility he could be reinstated" (Miletich & Sullivan, 2011, February 16, para. 43). He also said that "there are no grounds for Birk to be decommissioned as a law-enforcement officer" (Miletich & Sullivan, 2011, February 16, para. 46). In an editorial in the police guild newsletter, O'Neill reviewed the proceedings of the inquest (which he had attended) and contended that the news coverage had been biased and the public's response unfair. He described Officer Birk's situation as "tragic" and talked of the collegial support that Birk might need at this adverse juncture in his career:

> I also would like to thank the many officers who came to the courtroom to support Officer Birk. I know that some felt that the department discouraged officers from attending, but I know that the show of support, especially from officers who had been involved in shooting situations in their careers meant a lot to Officer Birk and his family. (O'Neill, 2011, p. 2)

There were many reactions to the news reports (595 comments on one article), but the feelings being expressed proved surprisingly diverse. On the one hand, Birk, the prosecutor, and the state legislature received the unfavorable attention one would have predicted, but there were also disparate views. Some readers complained that other readers tended to react differently to incidents depending on the ethnicity of protagonists or that they responded only when harm had been done instead of considering effective or preventive action. In addition to these entries, many others were deleted, which meant that they had been adjudged to be over the top, unfair, or intemperate by site administrators.

ENGAGING THE POLICE CULTURE

The newly appointed head of a large corporation who was interviewed by *The New York Times* alluded as follows to his recruitment experience:

So I said to John, "Tell me about the culture." And John's response
was one of the reasons I took the job. He said, "Bob, if you're the CEO,
the culture's what you want it to be." And I thought about that, and it
really was motivating to me. Wouldn't it be an interesting challenge
to be able to more directly influence a culture? (Bryant, 2010, p. BN2)

In the 1960s, no liberal police chief who was of sound mind would
have considered making such a claim, but today some police chiefs (and
some city executives) might be tempted to take credit for redirecting
their departments to become more community oriented. Seattle's police
department might be a plausible candidate for such aspirations. The force
is nationally recruited, cosmopolitan, highly educated, and diverse. The
department's mission statement specifies as a premise that "*delivering
respectful police services* means treating people the way you want to be
treated" (Seattle Police Department, 2002, 1.040, emphasis in original)
and lists priorities such as the following:

> [To] foster an organizational culture where fundamental values are
> integrity, accountability, ethical decision making, and respect for civil
> and constitutional rights; . . . strengthen links with all community
> members through open communications, mutual responsibility, and a
> commitment to service; . . . [and] using a flexible problem-solving
> approach that achieves results. (Seattle Police Department, 2002, 1.040)

These statements of principle, and the kind of organization they describe,
deviate markedly from the images of the Seattle Police Department promulgated by some members of the chorus and memorialized in letters to the Justice Department. The discrepancy raises several possibilities: (a) The police
department's mission statement may be largely poetry and a public-relations
ploy; (b) the mission statement represents the wishful thinking of leaders of
the department but would not be subscribed to by the majority of its members; (c) the statement describes ideas that are being disseminated within the
organization and that are at present warmly endorsed by only a minority of
officers; (d) these statements are objectives that are being promulgated
within the department, which most members of the department would more
or less endorse; or (e) the statement accurately describes how every member
of the department feels and spells out what he or she wants to achieve.

In an editorial on February 17, 2011, *The Seattle Times* suggested that community-oriented principles had not been fully internalized in the ranks of the Seattle Police Department and that more reinforcement was needed from above:

> Remedial attention to minority relations in the community is plainly overdue. Mayor Mike McGinnis, teamed with Police Chief John Diaz, must push back against any departmental resistance to race and social-justice training. Such instruction is elemental to repairing existing tensions that only festered in the wake of the shooting. ("The Williams Shooting," 2011, February 17, para. 10)

CULTURAL DIVERSITY IN THE LOCKER ROOM

A great deal of new light was eventually shed on the "resistance" alluded to in the editorial and on the proposal to address this resistance with additional "race and social-justice training." There was a sequence of news stories about a chain of events that had its inception several weeks earlier.

On January 27, 2011, an account of a public meeting appeared in *The Stranger,* a newspaper that is available in kiosks across the city of Seattle (Madrid, 2011). The meeting was one in which Chief Diaz had acted as guest speaker to talk about crime prevention. A member of the audience had asked the chief to comment about a controversial op-ed essay that had reportedly appeared in *The Guardian,* the police guild's newsletter. The chief characterized the contribution as unhelpful but also said that officers have first amendment rights to express unhelpful views in their spare time.

Once the question and response surfaced, additional details emerged. The source of the comments in the newsletter was said to be a veteran officer who had previously described himself as a "libertarian," concerned about encroachments of government in the lives of citizens. The encroachments the officer had discussed in *The Guardian* were the self-same race and social justice initiative and training, which he characterized as "a socialist scheme that judges people not as individuals but by their race, ethnicity, and socioeconomic status" (Pomper, 2011, cited in Thomas, 2011, para. 5). The officer asked in his commentary, "At what point do we say, 'Hell no!' to the indoctrination?" (Pomper, 2011, cited in Thomas, 2011, para. 12). He indicated that a boycott of a "de-policing" course might not be the place to draw the line, because attendance "served as a good way to learn what the enemy is up to" (Pomper, 2011, cited in Thomas, 2011, para. 15). He suggested that refusing to participate in a compulsory race-relations survey might serve as a good starting point (Pomper, 2011, cited in Thomas, 2011).

The full text of the officer's *Guardian* column was ultimately widely circulated and inspired any number of angry rejoinders, including a column titled "Seattle Police Officer, It's Time to Turn in Your Badge" (Large, 2011). The mayor was also quoted by several sources as expressing a comparable sentiment.[1] In his President's Message, O'Neill indirectly responded by inquiring, "Where is the ACLU [American Civil Liberties Union]?" (O'Neill, 2011, p. 2). He also wrote:

> I wonder why some in city government have such a hard time believing that city employees may not share their political ideals. I have a news flash for these folks; we have officers who listen to Rush Limbaugh and Glenn Beck religiously! I know it is hard to believe but we have officers, armed with guns, who not only vote republican in every election, but they [also] drive "gas-guzzling 4 × 4s" with gun racks and NRA [National Rifle Association] stickers on the bumpers! I'm not kidding, it is true! Some of them even attend church regularly. . . . But you know what is also true? We have officers who listen to NPR [National Public Radio], believe Al Gore, contribute to liberal causes, and loathe SUVs. Do you want to know something else? Both types of officers proudly serve the citizens of Seattle! They are able to check their personal opinions and politics at the door and do their job. (O'Neill, 2011, p. 2)

O'Neill's paean to diversity looked appropriately presidential and commendably eloquent, but it might have missed the key question, which was not whether there were conservatives (including Tea Party conservatives) in

---

[1] The mayor's office may have taken umbrage at being described as a "quaint socialist cabal" by a city employee (Pomper, as cited in Thomas, 2011).

the ranks but whether officers in the Seattle Police Department subscribed to its community-oriented mission or were disposed to subvert it.

SHAPING A CULTURE FROM BELOW

On the face of it, *The Seattle Times* suggestion that the department redouble its training efforts to overcome resistance sounded sensible, but it would not be a promising approach to reaching an officer who had defined his training experience as compulsory brainwashing.[2] At minimum, it would appear that the contents of training might stand revisiting, to prevent unfairly jaundiced and off-putting interpretations. This need for clarification was highlighted by a second contribution to *The Guardian*, in which an officer addressed the mayor of Seattle as follows:

> Can your city survive one officer who is of the opinion that "social justice" is incompatible with justice being equally applied? I sure hope so, because I can assure you that there is more than just one officer who feels that way in the Seattle Police Department, [myself] included. My job is to apply the law equally and fairly, not to ensure what you might define as a "socially just" outcome. (Stoltz, 2011, p. 4)

The idea of a dialogue with a participant who had shown a predilection for hurling ad hominem assaults might appear uninviting. However, even challenging targets are often worth the effort that can be involved in reaching them. In this case, the officer was—and presumably continues to be—a contributing member of the department and a source of peer influence. He had served as field training officer for six years, which made him a formative agent for young members of the organization. He was recognized for expertise, having been mountain-bike patrol coordinator for his precinct. He had been a member of a community police team. Last, the man is on record as favoring the benevolent exercise of police discretion,

---

[2] The father of social psychology, Kurt Lewin, was fond of pointing out that attempts to produce change by adding to driving forces in a force field were apt to promote increases in resisting forces and to create tension. He suggested that the problem can be avoided by incorporating sources of resistance in the process of planning change (Lewin, 1947).

having written a booklet subtitled "A Cop's Inside Scoop on Avoiding Traffic Tickets" (Pomper, 2007).[3]

It would obviously not be promising or appropriate to engage this officer in political debate, but he could profitably participate in an examination of questions devoid of ideological import, such as, How can the department counter the impression that we engage in profiling? Are there differences in problems posed for the police in different precincts that we need to take into account? How should the department accommodate these differences? How can you reach members of the community who are afraid of the police? How does one reassure citizens who feel that they have been unfairly singled out for attention? How do you handle a situation where citizens have limited knowledge of English? What do you do when another officer appears to be losing his cool in an altercation? What do you do when a citizen appears to be losing his cool?

So-called racial and social justice questions, by other names, can boil down to criteria that officers must use in exercising discretion. These questions are implicit in practical problems that officers face every day to which they need to respond. The discussion of such problems has to draw on the thinking of officers who are actively out on patrol, but it could profitably include any number of participants, including the member of the police guild board of directors who is "a certified instructor in the Profiling in Policing class" (O'Neill, 2011, p. 2). In groups addressing such issues, one would also want to include experienced line supervisors and instructors in the training academy.

The Seattle Police Department has a history of being receptive to planning efforts from its rank-and-file members. The original concept of bicycle patrols originated in Seattle with Police Officer Paul Grady two decades ago. There are also other instances in the history of the Seattle Police Department of amenability to ideas from below. This receptivity is not surprising because community-oriented policing at its best is also officer-oriented policing.

---

[3] According to a biographical passage provided to Amazon.com, the book

is written for motorists who want to know how to behave if they get stopped by a cop for a traffic violation, that may improve their chances of getting a warning. Or to at least make them less likely to talk or act themselves into a citation. (Pomper, n.d.)

This point has been eloquently made by Herman Goldstein (1987), the originator of problem-oriented policing, who argued for "greater involvement of rank-and-file officers in the development of community policing" (p. 14). Goldstein wrote:

> If properly coordinated, the changes contemplated in community policing can have great appeal to these officers. . . . They value independence, which enables them to make greater use of their talents and experience. They appreciate opportunities to develop more positive relationships with the community, to enhance their status, and to derive greater work satisfaction. The "common sense" aspects of community policing, which receive the enthusiastic support of police officers, and the values an agency seeks to develop in implementing community policing often happily coincide. (p. 14)

The message in the medium can therefore be that the sum of facilitated involvements by dedicated officers who have freely decided to buy into reform is the very opposite of change that can be described as imposed from above. A participatory reform strategy can lead to the formation of an officer culture that is supportive of change—and whatever that process is called, it does not lend itself to being characterized as indoctrination by a socialist elite.

Putting hyperbole aside, the shape of top-down change implementation can distract police officers from the substance and can blind them to available opportunities for personal development. Sadd and Grinc (1996) surveyed police departments in eight cities where innovative reforms had been introduced. They reported:

> Most of the officers interviewed felt that community policing was happening *to* them rather than *with* them and that there was no attempt to involve the rank and file in decision making. . . . [Officers] were almost unanimous in criticizing what they saw as heavy-handed implementation by management. Community policing emphasizes community empowerment and involves citizens in decision making. Rank-and-file patrol officers, however, generally argued that administrators had excluded them from decision making. (p. 11)

Such feelings are apt to lead to the cynical conclusion that "all new projects are driven by political pressures on police and city managers and are thus inherently of dubious value" (p. 11).

THE CHORUS AND POLICE REFORM

Any planning to be done by the Seattle Police Department in March 2011 had to be put on hold—at least temporarily—by developments that had been germinating behind the scenes. These developments had been instigated by sentiments from the chorus. *The New York Times* gave due credit to the power of public opinion in a story on April 1, 2011, which reported the following:

> The Justice Department said Thursday that it would conduct a comprehensive investigation of the Seattle Police Department after a series of episodes in which police officers have been accused of using unnecessary force and discriminating against minorities. The decision follows a preliminary investigation . . . amid a *public backlash* [emphasis added] after an officer shot and killed a wood carver who was a member of First Nations tribe of Canada. . . . The killing followed other problems with the police over the past year that have *rattled this city* [emphasis added]. (Yardley, 2011, p. A17)

In a letter announcing the impending investigation, the attorney general's office specified that "we will seek to determine whether there are *systemic* [emphasis added] violations of the Constitution or laws of the United States by sworn law enforcement officers of the SPD [Seattle Police Department]" (Perez, 2011, para. 2). This objective reflected the suspicions voiced by some members of the chorus, but any serious chance that systemic problems might be uncovered was not widely regarded as likely, given the enlightened leadership of Seattle and its police department.

The Justice Department's announcement was described by the leadership of Seattle as a challenge rather than a threat. The focus in official comments was on passages in the letter that promised "to provide recommendations on ways to improve police practices, when appropriate. . . . [and to] identify any financial, technical, or other assistance the United States may be able to provide to assist the city in correcting the identified deficiencies" (Perez, 2011, para. 2). Chief Diaz was quoted as telling the editorial board of *The Seattle Times* that he welcomed a "free audit from the Department of Justice" (Carter, 2011, para. 4). Sargent O'Neill, the union president, characterized the investigation as auspicious. He said, "In a way I'm looking forward to this . . . they may come up with suggestions in ways we could do better in both areas [use of force and biased enforcement]" (Carter, 2011, para. 27–28).

A succession of unfortunate incidents and angry responses to these incidents had alerted the police leadership (including the city administration and the union) to the need for and inevitability of reform. The chorus had made its contributions by pointing to critical incidents, communicating urgency, cementing motivation, and exerting and maintaining pressure. The choruses of the sixties had played a comparable role as bystanders to incidents who irritated officers through their perceived unsolicited interference. Then as now, the crowd had been the engine of reform, making the status quo ante increasingly untenable.

Crowds may have played a consistent role as instigators of change, but crowds have not been noted for contributions to the planning of change. Some chorus members in Seattle stood out for the erudition of their comments, but complaints are primarily a vehicle for expressing feelings and detailing concerns. Crowds have usually been described in the literature as "irrational." However, the fairness of this characterization depends on what one means by rationality (Milgram & Toch, 1969). Crowds—including the virtual crowds of today—offer opportunities for ventilating shared legitimate concerns that provide a rationale for change. Change as such, however, is best accomplished by social movements that emerge out of crowds, and by organizations.

In the case of Seattle, the reform that was to take place could eventually be shaped by members of the police department—hopefully, with the participation of every segment of the department—in collaboration with citizen groups that are truly representative of the community, with the skilled assistance of dispassionate and empathetic agents of change. It can be a difficult and exciting task, but thanks to the chorus, conditions appear ripe for its accomplishment.

THREE

EPILOGUE

10

Volatile Scenarios in the Ghetto

The Kerner Commission, writing in 1968, alluded to a

> bitter social debate over law enforcement . . . [in which] one side, dis-
> turbed and perplexed by sharp rises in crime and urban violence, exerts
> extreme pressure on police for tougher law enforcement. Another
> group, inflamed against police as agents of repression, tends toward
> defiance of what it regards as order maintenance at the expense of jus-
> tice. (National Advisory Commission on Civil Disorders, 1968, p. 157)

This "bitter social debate" is one that continues unabated to this day and
might not be closer to resolution than it was five decades or so ago. One
source of the bitterness—both today and in the past—is that the "pressure
for tougher enforcement" has inspired police departments to initiate a disproportionate number of citizen contacts in minority neighborhoods, a
practice that has added the term *profiling* to our lexicon.[1]

---

[1] There are indications that other disadvantaged minorities may have been subjected to disproportionate
stop-and-frisks. Barrett (1998) referred to a 1915 opinion alluding to a police officer who was accidentally
shot while "engaged in searching Italians" (pp. 758–759).

In its day, the Kerner Commission had to deal with the riots of the period and the fact that "many of the serious disturbances took place in cities whose police [we]re among the . . . most professional in the country" (National Advisory Commission on Civil Disorders, 1968, p. 158). The commission speculated that among the reasons for this counterintuitive finding could be that "professional" departments "may simply be using law enforcement methods that increase the total volume of police contacts with the public" (National Advisory Commission on Civil Disorders, 1968, p. 158). Of particular relevance, wrote the commission in its report, might be "practices, sometimes known a 'preventive aggressive patrol' . . . [that] involve a large number of police–citizen contacts initiated by police rather than in response to a call for help or service" (National Advisory Commission on Civil Disorders, 1968, p. 159). In describing these contacts, the commission alluded to

> "stop-and-frisk" or field interrogation reports . . . [that were expected from patrol officers, noting that the] pressure to produce . . . may lead to widespread use of these techniques without adequate differentiation between genuinely suspicious behavior and behavior which is suspicious to a particular officer merely because it is unfamiliar. (National Advisory Commission on Civil Disorders, 1968, p. 159)[2]

It is ironic that stop-and-frisk reports such as those the commission alluded to continue to provide ammunition for debate. In relation to such reports, a court in 2008 ordered the release of "all data except the names and contact information of individuals who were stopped by the [New York City] police and the names of the reporting and reviewing officers" (*Floyd v. City of New York*, 2008, p. 13). Analysis of the information led to the conclusion that "most stops occur in Black and Hispanic neighborhoods, and the main factor for determining who gets stopped is race" (Center for Constitutional Rights, 2010a, p. 1). A *New York Times* editorial that was based on the information extrapolated as follows:

---

[2] The "pressure to produce" the Kerner Commission presciently alluded to has been extraordinarily exacerbated since the introduction of computers in police departments to provide disaggregated productivity indexes, which are then punitively publicized (under the fashionable COMPSTAT [COMPuter STATistics or COMParative STATistics] managerial model) to castigate middle managers for the allegedly substandard productivity of subordinates who have not stopped-and-frisked their assigned share of "suspicious" civilians.

If the number of stops keeps going up—and officers begin to be seen as acting recklessly and unfairly—the department will risk permanently alienating an entire generation of people in the very neighborhoods where trust in the law is most needed. ("Lingering Questions," 2010, p. A26)

The Kerner Commission had mentioned that the targeting of young Black men in particular—especially of young Black men in groups—was bound to invite angry resistance and contribute to the perpetuation of hostility to the police. The Commission added that the overaggressive behavior of individual officers could exacerbate the situation and indicated that "in assessing the impact of police misconduct, we emphasize that the improper acts of a relatively few officers may create severe tensions between the department and the entire Negro community" (National Advisory Commission on Civil Disorders, 1968, p. 159).

SUPPORTIVE DOCUMENTATION

The Kerner Commission sponsored several formal studies in the sixties, including a survey of police officers in 15 metropolitan areas. A published report summarized the views of officers in 11 of these cities and confirmed that "a lack of public support . . . is the policeman's major complaint" (Groves, 1968, p. 103). The report also pointed to the "in-group solidarity" of police officers, which the authors speculated "most likely exacerbates the already marked hostility" between citizens and police (Groves, 1968, p. 103).

The citizen side of the equation was explored in a survey by a University of Michigan team that was also sponsored by the Kerner Commission (Campbell & Schuman, 1968). The researchers asked whether police frisk or search people without good reason. Over a third of Black respondents indicated that such searches took place in their neighborhood. A similarly substantial proportion of Black respondents alleged that "police rough up people unnecessarily when they are arresting them or afterwards" (Campbell & Schuman, 1968, p. 43). The reported figure was even higher among respondents in their teens (49%) and in their twenties (43%), whereas fully over half of the youths said that police "don't show respect for people and use insulting language" or that they search people without justification (Campbell & Schuman, 1968, p. 44).

CONTINUED DISPARITIES IN EXPERIENCE

Recent studies have pointed to the timelessness of the documentation commissioned by the Kerner Commission and have suggested that, in some respects, the situation across the country has deteriorated. A national survey of adults in metropolitan areas (Weitzer & Tuch, 2004) highlighted the following response differences, among others:

- When asked whether they had been stopped by the police on the street in their city for no good reason, one third of Black respondents (34%) answered in the affirmative, compared with 13% of Whites.
- Three fourths (75%) of Black respondents reported that police treat Black citizens worse than Whites; three fourths of Whites saw no difference in treatment.
- Almost half of Black respondents (48%) maintained that police in their city often used excessive force; only 13% of Whites concurred.
- Forty-six percent of Blacks (as opposed to 8% of Whites) thought that racial or ethnic prejudice was "very common" among police in their city.
- Forty-three percent of Blacks (and only 3% of Whites) said that they recalled feeling that "they were stopped by the police just because of their race or as ethnic background."

In a recapitulation of their report, Weitzer and Tuch (2006) concluded:

> These racial disparities are *not simply a matter of opinion.* Contrasting perceptions of police misconduct reflect, at least to some extent, real differences in police practices across different kinds of neighborhoods, judging from research based on police record and on systematic observations of officers on the streets. . . . Both these studies and our respondents' self-reports indicate that *at the neighborhood level, police misconduct is largely confined to disadvantaged neighborhood communities.* (pp. 55–56, emphasis in the original)

The misconduct alluded to primarily has had to do with the pressure to "produce" which leads to the wholesale interception of citizens going about their business in minority neighborhoods. In an op-ed essay dated February 2, 2010, the *New York Times* columnist Bob Herbert thus reported that "people going about their daily business, bothering no one, are menaced out of the blue by the police, forced to spread a car, to be searched" (p. A27). He wrote that "people who object to the harassment are often threatened with arrest" (B. Herbert, 2010, February 2, p. A27). Elsewhere, the columnist reported that "when you listen to people who have been subjected to this relentless harassment, you get a sense of the awful personal consequences. People are made to feel low, intimidated, worthless, helpless. They dread the very sight of the police" (B. Herbert, 2010, July 6, p. A23).

B. Herbert acknowledged that "the Police Department . . . [has] said repeatedly that the racial makeup of the people stopped and frisked is proportionately similar to the racial makeup of people committing crimes" (B. Herbert, 2010, February 2, p. A27). He appropriately concluded, however, that "the fact that a certain percentage of criminals may be Black or Hispanic is no reason for the police to harass individuals from those groups when there is no indication whatever that they have done anything wrong" (B. Herbert, 2010, February 2, p. A27). Bobb, Miller, Davis, and Root (2006) pointed out that, as a matter of definition,

> It *is* racial profiling when broad statistical correlations are used as a basis of focusing suspicion on a given individual; i.e., more Latino than white teenagers are arrested for street crimes, therefore that specific Latino teenager in this high crime area should be checked out. (p. 32, emphasis in the original)

REINFORCEMENT FROM THE SUPREME COURT

Michael Tonry (2011) has noted:

> In principle, police should stop citizens only when individualized bases exist—that satisfy legal requirements of proof—to believe they have been involved in a crime. In practice, especially in minority areas of cities, those restraints are honored only in the breach. (p. 142)

Allegations that police search citizens without justification reached the U.S. Supreme Court twice during its 1968 term. By this time in the Warren Court's history, a series of groundbreaking decisions had alarmed the more conservative segments of the community, who were vehemently obsessed with the notion of an unprecedented crime wave. In street-level law enforcement circles, the Court had acquired the reputation of having invented "rights" that handcuffed the police and paralyzed the criminal justice system (see Chapter 4, this volume). This jaundiced conception of the Court's contribution rested on two of the Court's decisions in the early sixties: one relating to a right to counsel during questioning following arrest and the second to the inadmissibility of evidence obtained in searches not authorized by warrant or a recognized exception to the warrant requirement.

The disgruntlement in police circles was not tempered by the fact that neither of these Supreme Court opinions had much of a bearing on most police–citizen encounters, such as those described in Chapters 2 and 3. Street interrogations and minor misdemeanor arrests rarely led to prosecutions and trials, where legal representation and the inadmissibility of evidence would be at issue. And when in 1968 the Supreme Court was presented with questions related to mundane and prevalent police activities, such as street interrogations, the disgruntled critics hardly noticed that the Court's opinions in these cases substantially facilitated rather than impeded prevailing practices.

TERRY AND THE UNFETTERED TERRY STOP

The more salient of the two cases was *Terry v. Ohio* (1968), decided on June 10, and signed by Chief Justice Earl Warren. The encounter that sparked the litigation was initiated as follows:

> Officer McFadden testified that while he was patrolling in plain clothes in downtown Cleveland at approximately 2:30 in the afternoon of October 31, 1963, his attention was attracted by two men, Chilton and Terry, standing on the corner of Huron Road and Euclid Avenue. He had never seen the two men before, and he was unable to say precisely what first drew his attention to them. However, he testified that he had been a policeman for 39 years. . . . He explained that

he had developed routine habits of observation over the years. . . . He added: "Now in this case when I looked over they didn't look right to me." (*Terry v. Ohio*, 1968, p. 5)[3]

The officer's suspicions grew when the objects of his attention inspected a store window, which suggested to him that the duo might be contemplating a break-in. Based on this premise, the officer intercepted the men (plus a third man) and searched their "outer garments" as a precautionary move, finding two of the three men in possession of guns.

Chief Justice Warren wrote the following in assessing the reasonableness of suspicion, which was the Court's proposed criterion for the legitimacy of a stop-and-frisk:

> The police officer must be able to point to specific and articulable facts which, taken together with rational inferences from those facts, reasonably warrant that intrusion. . . . And in making that assessment it is imperative that the facts be judged against an objective standard: Would the facts available to the officer at the moment of seizure or search "warrant a man of reasonable caution in the belief" that the action taken was appropriate . . . [that intrusions could not be justified] based on nothing more substantial than inarticulate hunches . . . [and that] simple good faith on the part of the arresting officers is not enough. (*Terry v. Ohio*, 1968, p. 21–22)

Given these reassuring but subjective criteria, Chief Justice Warren found Officer McFadden's intervention to be reasonable, noting that "it would have been poor police work indeed for an officer of 30 years' experience in the detection of thievery from stores in the same neighborhood to have failed to investigate this behavior further" (*Terry v. Ohio*, 1968, p. 23). As to McFcadden's search for weapons, Warren wrote that the officer was entitled to protect himself:

> Certainly it would be unreasonable to require that police officers take unreasonable risks in the performance of their duties. American

---

[3] Nowhere in the *Terry* opinion is there mention of the fact that the men who aroused McFadden's suspicion happened to be young Black males.

criminals have a long tradition of armed violence, and every year in this country many law enforcement officers are killed in the line of duty, and thousands more are wounded. Virtually all of these deaths and a substantial portion of the injuries are inflicted with guns and knives. (*Terry v. Ohio*, 1968, pp. 23–24)

In reaching conclusions that generations of police officers have since relied on to conduct stop-and-frisks, the Court paid surprisingly little attention to the possible consequences of its formulation. As a general caveat, Chief Justice Warren noted that "under our decision, courts still retain their traditional responsibility to guard against police conduct that is overbearing or harassing, or which trenches upon personal security without the objective evidentiary justification that the Constitution requires" (*Terry v. Ohio*, 1968, p. 15). But in a footnote (11), the Court acknowledged that street interrogations had become a source of friction with minority groups and "exacerbated police–community tensions" (*Terry v. Ohio*, 1968). In another footnote (14), the Court noted that "the degree of community resentment aroused by particular practices is clearly relevant to an assessment of the quality of the intrusion" (*Terry v. Ohio*, 1968).[4]

The *Terry* opinion was accompanied by a vigorous dissent from Justice Douglas, who could not understand how an intervention could be constitutional "unless there was probable cause to believe that (1) a crime had been committed or (2) a crime was in the process of being committed or (3) a crime was about to be committed" (*Terry v. Ohio*, 1968, p. 35). Justice Douglas wrote that "the term 'probable cause' rings a bell of certainty that is not sounded by phrases such as 'reasonable suspicion'" (*Terry v. Ohio*, 1968, p. 37). He concluded by hypothesizing that the opinion had to be read against the context of the intense concern with crime and violence during this period. He ended with the eminently quotable declaration, "There have been powerful hydraulic pressures throughout

---

[4] Maclin (1998) noted:

> Regrettably . . . the Court's disquiet about the racial consequences of stop and frisk policies was buried under a lengthy discussion of the exclusionary rule, and clearly occupied a subordinate position to the Court's overriding concern about police safety and violent crime. (p. 1285)

our history that bear heavily on the Court to water down constitutional guarantees and give the police the upper hand," and he asserted that "the hydraulic pressure has probably never been greater than it is today" (*Terry v. Ohio*, 1968, p. 39).[5]

UNLEASHING THE NEW YORK CITY POLICE

Concurrently with *Terry v. Ohio* (1968), the Court announced its decision in two related cases, *Sibron v. State of New York* and *Peters v. New York* (1968). Sibron was less seminal than Terry but arguably may have proved equally consequential, because in Sibron the Court decided not to question the provisions under which the New York Police Department had been conducting, and has continued to conduct, its increasingly controversial stop-and-frisk operations. If Sibron did not open a Pandora's box, it handily served to keep it open.

Sibron is named after a man who was convicted after being stopped and searched by New York City police officers. This individual had been under observation for eight hours, during which an officer saw him conversing with other persons the officer "knew from past experience were narcotics addicts" (*Sibron v. State of New York, Peters v. State of New York,* 1968). Exhausted from these conversations,

> [Sibron entered a restaurant,] sat down and ordered a pie and coffee, and, as he was eating, [the officer] approached him and told him to come outside. Once outside, the officer said to Sibron, "You know what I am after." According to the officer, Sibron "mumbled something and

---

[5] Justice Douglas was not the only member of the Court to experience premonitions. Barrett (1998) quoted from a long letter Justice Brennan addressed to the Chief Justice, in which he wrote:

> I've become acutely concerned that the mere fact of our affirmance in Terry will be taken by the police all over the country as our license for them to carry on, indeed widely expand, present "aggressive surveillance" techniques which the press tells us are being deliberately employed in Miami, Chicago, Detroit and other ghetto cities. This is happening, of course, in response to the "crime in the streets" alarums being sounded in this election year in the Congress, the White House, and every Governor's office. . . . In this lies the terrible risk that police will conjure up "suspicious circumstances" and courts will credit their versions. It will not take much of this to aggravate the already white heat resentment of ghetto Negroes against the police—and the Court will become the scapegoat. . . . If we are to affirm Terry, I think the tone of our opinion may be even more important than what we say. (pp. 825–826)

reached into his pocket." Simultaneously, [the officer] thrust his hand into the same pocket, discovering several glassine envelopes, which, it turned out, contained heroin. (*Sibron v. State of New York, Peters v. State of New York*, 1968, p. 45)

Sibron was convicted and sentenced to six months in jail. His case was combined with that of a second appellant, Peters, who had been convicted of possessing burglary tools under circumstances evincing an intent to employ them in the commission of a crime. Peters had been apprehended by Officer Lasky in the apartment building in which the officer lived. Officer Lasky had observed Peters and another man skulking about, looking furtive:

[The officer went out of his apartment,] entered the hallway and slammed the door loudly behind him. This precipitated a flight down the stairs on the part of the two men, and Officer Lasky gave chase. His apartment was on the sixth floor, and he apprehended Peters between the fourth and fifth floors. Grabbing Peters by the collar, he continued down another flight in unsuccessful pursuit of the other man. (*Sibron v. State of New York, Peters v. State of New York*, 1968, p. 49)

Peters claimed to have been courting a resident lady but indicated that he was too much of a gentleman to reveal her name. Officer Lasky, however, noticed a lump in Peters's pocket and investigated. His search yielded the burglary tools. The judge who sentenced Peters concurred with Lasky's view that it would be suspicious "for a man to tiptoe about in the public hall of an apartment house while on a visit to his unidentified girlfriend, and when observed by another tenant, to rapidly descend by stairway in the presence of elevators" (*Sibron v. State of New York, Peters v. State of New York*, 1968, p. 49). Peters turned out to be a repeat offender and was convicted of a felony.

ONE YES, ONE NO, AND TWO DIVERGENT VIEWS

The Supreme Court reversed Sibron's conviction (he had already served his term in jail) on the ground that the officer had lacked reasonable suspicion in that "the inference that persons who talk to narcotics addicts are engaged in the criminal traffic in narcotics is simply not the sort of reasonable inference required to support an intrusion by the police upon an individual's personal security" (*Sibron v. State of New York, Peters v. State of New York*, 1968, p. 62). The "intrusion" the Court was alluding to was the officer's hand in Sibron's pocket (the search), not the officer's interruption of Sibron's dinner (the stop).

The Court noted that the state's stop-and-frisk law provided that "when a police officer has stopped a person for questioning . . . and reasonably suspects that he is in danger of life or limb, he may search such a person for a dangerous weapon" (*Sibron v. State of New York, Peters v. State of New York*, 1968, p. 43), but the Court suggested that in this case, the officer's "opening statement—'You know what I am after'"—did not sound as if he were talking about a dangerous weapon (*Sibron v. State of New York, Peters v. State of New York*, 1968, p. 64).

The Court decided not to address the question of whether Sibron (or a Sibron equivalent) could have been stopped (and questioned) under the authority of the statute that provided

> a police officer may stop any person abroad in a public place whom he reasonably suspects is committing, has committed, or is about to commit a felony . . . and may demand of him his name, address, and an explanation of his activities. (*Sibron v. State of New York, Peters v. State of New York*, 1968, p. 44)

The Court did note in passim that these provisions left open questions such as what the officer could do "in the event of a refusal to answer or even whether the interrogation following the 'stop' is 'custodial'" (*Sibron v. State of New York, Peters v. State of New York*, 1968, p. 61). However, the Court's inattention to such mundane details was not shared by Justice Fortas, who added a concurring opinion in which he stated, "There must be something at least in the activities of the person being observed or in his surroundings that affirmatively suggests particular criminal activity, completed, current, or intended" (*Sibron v. State of New York, Peters v. State of New York*, 1968, p. 73). Justice Fortas did not think that the observed conversations of Sibron fit this definition.

From the other wing of the bench, Justice Black registered an impassioned dissent with respect to the review of Sibron's search:

> Law enforcement officers all over the Nation have gained little protection from the courts through opinions here if they are left helpless to act in self defense when a man associating intimately and continuously with addicts, upon meeting an officer, shifts his hand immediately to a pocket where weapons are constantly carried. . . . This Court, sitting in the marble halls of the Supreme Court Building in Washington, DC, should be most cautious. (*Sibron v. State of New York, Peters v. State of New York,* 1968, pp. 81–82)

As we shall see, time would show that Justice Black need not have worried, because the Court has been bending over backward to support the flimsiest justifications for police officers to stop and question residents of minority neighborhoods.

THE FRUITS OF REASONABLE SUSPICION

An authoritative study of New York Police Department data was released to the press in October 2010 and presented mind-boggling statistics about New York City police stop-and-frisks:

> In 2008, the number of people stopped and frisked was 540,302. In 2009, it was 576,394 . . . a 6.7% increase in one year and almost a 600% increase since 2002. In 2009 . . . 84 percent of [those stopped] were Black and Latin residents, although they comprise only 26 and 27 percent of New York City total population respectively. The year 2009 was not an anomaly. (Center for Constitutional Rights, 2010a, p. 1)

Of the persons who were stopped and questioned by the New York City police, a relatively small minority (6%) were detained to be charged with an offense. Only one out of 100 (1.1% of Black detainees, 1.7 % of Whites) was found to carry a weapon. This miniscule yield is particularly interesting given that the reiterated objective of the stop-and-frisk sweeps has been to "get guns off the street" to "prevent violent crime" (Center for Constitutional Rights, 2010a).

Officers have to record a reason for stopping a citizen. Their most frequently listed reason has been "furtive movement." This is not a justification that detained citizens would find easy to accept, and the possibility that citizens might often have unresolved questions about why they were being stopped makes it unremarkable that stop-and-frisk officers report that in one of four interceptions they have had to resort to force. The use of "hands" is the most frequent modality of force recorded by the police (in one of every five stops; Center for Constitutional Rights, 2010a).

THE POLICE-AVERSIVE CITIZEN

The invoking of furtive movements raises the question of what "movements" one might reasonably expect—especially among young Black men stalked by menacing contingents of officers. A former member of the New York police force observed in a letter to the editors of *The New York Times* that "for too many minority New Yorkers, the sight of a passing police car brings a sense of dread and angst" (O'Donnell, 2010). Such a sentiment plausibly finds expression in evasive movement, which officers can point to as a presumptive index of culpability. The resulting interceptions (stop-and-frisks) are bound to increase—and disseminate—the "dread and angst," especially among out-of-shape citizens who have learned not to overestimate their own capacity for taking evasive action.

The question of what inferences a police officer might legitimately draw from a citizen's precipitant departure was covered in some detail in a Supreme Court opinion (*Illinois v. Wardlow,* 2000) and in an eloquent dissent drafted by Justice Stevens.

Chief Justice Rehnquist delivered the opinion in this case and drew the following conclusion about evasive behavior as legitimate grounds for interception:

> Our cases have . . . recognized that nervous, evasive behavior is a pertinent factor in determining reasonable suspicion. . . . Headlong flight—wherever it occurs—is a consummate act of evasion: It is not necessarily indicative of wrongdoing, but it is certainly suggestive of such. . . . Unprovoked flight is simply not a mere refusal to cooperate.

Flight, by its very nature, is "not going about one's business"; in fact, it is just the opposite. (*Illinois v. Wardlow*, 2000, p. 125)

Justice Stevens—in his dissent—responded as follows:

The question in this case concerns "the degree of suspicion that attaches to" a person's flight—or, more precisely, what "common sense" conclusions can be drawn respecting the motives behind that flight. A pedestrian may break into a run for a variety of reasons—to catch up with a friend a block or two away, to seek shelter from an impending storm, to arrive at a bus stop before the bus leaves, to get home in time for dinner, to resume jogging after a pause for rest, to avoid contact with a bore or a bully, or simply to answer the call of nature—any of which might coincide with the arrival of an officer in the vicinity. A pedestrian might also run because he or she has just sighted one or more police officers. (*Illinois v. Wardlow*, 2000, pp. 128–129)

With respect to citizens who flee at the sight of police officers, Justice Stevens added the following:

Among some citizens, particularly minorities and those residing in high crime areas, there is also the possibility that the fleeing person is entirely innocent, but, with or without justification, believes that contact with the police can itself be dangerous, apart from any criminal activity associated with the officer's sudden presence. (*Illinois v. Wardlow*, 2000, p. 132)

Stevens pointed out that given the obvious and well-known fact that police gravitate to high-crime areas and that therefore denizens of such areas might feel exposed and vulnerable to indiscriminate police interventions, "the character of the neighborhood arguably makes an inference of guilt *less* [emphasis added] appropriate, rather than more so" (*Illinois v. Wardlow*, 2000, p. 139). This point happens to be of pressing relevance because police officers tend to cite a person's "location in a high crime area" as their clinching argument for stopping and interrogating him—particularly if he or she has "furtively" moved. Most residents of high-crime areas happen to be law abiding but are forced to live in almost commensurate fear of criminals and of the police who seem unable to distinguish victims from victimizers. Such residents would understandably seek to avoid the police—not because they were criminals but because they would not want to be treated as such. And because location is correlated with ethnicity, such residents might also conclude that they have been the target of racial profiling by the police.

Despite the consistent emphasis on the psychological meaning of efforts to escape, in at least one decision related to stop-and-frisks, the Supreme Court alluded to "slowing down" rather than "running away" as the behavior that could provide grounds for reasonable suspicion. The Court added, however, that suspicious deceleration as a furtive movement must be considered in context. The opinion (delivered by Chief Justice Rehnquist) noted the following:

> We think it quite reasonable that a driver's slowing down, stiffening a posture, and failure to acknowledge a sighted law enforcement officer might well be unremarkable in one instance (such as a busy San Francisco highway) while quite unusual in another (such as a remote portion of rural southeastern Arizona).
>
> [The officer] was entitled to make an assessment of the situation in light of his specialized training and familiarity with the customs of the area's inhabitants. (*United States v. Arvizu*, 2002, p. 9)

The opinion reiterated:

> We have said repeatedly that [reviewing courts] must look at the "totality of circumstances" of each case. . . . This process allows officers to draw on their own experience and specialized training to make inferences from and deductions about the cumulative information available to them that "might elude an untrained person." (*United States v. Arvizu*, 2002, p. 7)

The allusions to "experience" and "specialized training" make it ironic that officers with the most limited experience and training, such as officers who have recently graduated from the academy, tend to be assigned to stop-and-frisk sweeps in New York City. There may also be a question about the extent to which an officer's experience is a product of his own actions in the setting in which sweeps are conducted. In New York City, for example, one delimited target area has been Brownsville, Brooklyn, where 52,000 police stops had been recorded in 4 years. According to the report in the *New York Times*,

> To many residents here, the flood of young officers who roam the community each day are not equipped to make the subtle judgments required to tell one young man in low-hanging jeans concealing a weapon from another young man wearing similar clothes on his way to school. . . . Oddly, years ago when crime was higher, relations with the police seemed better, several residents said. The officers seemed to show a greater sense of who was law abiding and who was not, they said. Now, many residents say, the newer crop of officers seem to be more interested in small offenses than engaging the residents. (Rivera, Baker, & Roberts, 2010, p. A17)

There is in addition a question (which may be of particular interest to psychologists) of whether the cues relied on in formulating a "reasonable suspicion" based on the "totality of circumstances" can ever be reliably specified and accurately listed (as presupposed by the *Terry* decision) and whether they can ever be devoid of race-tinged stereotypes.[6] For example, according to one Brownsville resident, "When [the police] give a description, it's 'young man, black pants, blue shirt, black hat'. . . . That's mostly everybody" (Rivera, Baker, & Roberts, 2010, p. A17).

PROFILING AS THE CHORUS CONCERN OF THE FUTURE

The concerns of the chorus are once again those of the perceived unfairness, brutality, and discrimination of police interventions (see Chapter 1, this volume). These concerns nowadays tend to be embodied in complaints relating to profiling. Weitzer and Tuch (2006) thus reported:

---

[6] To the extent to which officers' past interventions may have been motivated by prejudice or based on stereotypes, their jaundiced encounters nonetheless make up the "experience" they can proudly cite in support of their future interventions. In this sense, experience can be the sum of well-rehearsed disasters or the fruit of replicated error.

Not only do most Americans reject racial profiling in principle, but they also see it as pervasive. The overwhelming majority of blacks (92 percent) and Hispanics (83 percent) believe that profiling is widespread in the United States. Most blacks (8 out of 10) and Hispanics (6 out of 10) also believe that profiling is pervasive in their own city, and a majority of blacks and near-majority of Hispanics see it as widespread in their own residential neighborhood. (pp. 83–84)

This scenario is ripe for a lament of the chorus. For a precedent, consider the following: "When he [a human] observes the laws of the land and the justice of the gods to which he has sworn, high stands his city; no city has he whom presumption leads to evil ways" (chorus of Antigone, cited in Kirkwood, 1954, p. 15). We have no reliable consensus as to "the justice of the gods," but some federal court will soon have to face the question of whether the modest offense-related yield of stop-and-frisk sweeps can reasonably justify the widespread psychological injury the strategy predictably engenders. The question for the police profession is more basic: It is whether the lessons of history (or of the prehistory of policing) have been sufficiently absorbed, given the ominous adage that those who do not attend to the past are fated to repeat it.

References

Abouhalkah, Y. T. (2010, June 16). Seattle cop's punch felt around the nation. *The Kansas City Star*. Retrieved from http://voices.kansascity.com/entries/seattle-cops-punch-felt-around-nation/

Alder, D. (2010, September 23). Inside look at Seattle Police training methods. *Maple Leaf Life*. Retrieved from http://www.mapleleaflife.com/2010/09/23/inside-look-at-seattle-police-training-methods/

Anderson, R. (2010, October 14). John T. Williams Inquest: Don't be surprised if his death is found unjustified. *The Daily Weekly*. Retrieved from http://blogs.seattleweekly.com/dailyweekly/2010/10/john_t_williams_court_inquest.php

Barrett, J. Q. (1998). Deciding the stop and frisk cases: A look inside the Supreme Court's conference. *St. John's Law Review, 72*, 749–890.

Bennett, C. B. (2010, June 21). Community outraged over police officer's punch of Black teen in the face. *blackvoicenews.com*. Retrieved from http://www.blackvoicenews.com/news/news-wire/44594-community-outraged-over-police-officers-punch-of-black-teen-in-the-face.html

Bhattacharjee, R. (2010, September 23). Council committee supports citizen involvement in firearms review board deliberations. *The Stranger*. Retrieved from http://slog.thestranger.com/slog/archives/2010/09/23/council-committee-supports-citizen-involvement-in-firearms-review-board-deliberations

Bittner, E. (1980). *The functions of the police in modern society: A review of background factors, current practices, and possible role models*. Cambridge, MA: Oelgeschlager, Gunn & Hain.

Black police organizations differ in opinion regarding punching incident. (2010, June 23). *The Seattle Medium*. Retrieved from http://www.seattlemedium.com/News/search/ArchiveContent.asp?NewsID=103854&sID=

Bobb, M. J., Miller, N. H., Davis, R. L., & Root, O. (2006). Racial profiling. In S. J. Muffler (Ed.), *Racial profiling: Issues, data, and analysis* (pp. 31–39). New York, NY: NOVA Science.

Bryant, A. (2010, December 26). Corner office: Robert Eckert. *The New York Times,* p. BN2.

Byron, L. (2010, November 18). Kicking video doesn't tell whole story, says Seattle PD union chief. *NWCN.com.* Retrieved from http://www.nwcn.com/news/washington/Kicking-video-doesnt-tell-whole-story-says-Seattle-PD-union-chief-109079289.html

Campbell, A., & Schuman, H. (1968). Racial attitudes in fifteen American cities. In National Advisory Commission on Civil Disorders (Ed.), *Supplemental studies for the National Advisory Commission on Civil Disorders* (pp. 1–67). Washington, DC: U.S. Government Printing Office.

Carter, M. (2011, March 31). Justice Department to investigate Seattle Police civil-rights practices. *The Seattle Times.* Retrieved from http://seattletimes.nwsource.com/html/localnews/2014648060_dojinvestigation01m.html

Carter, M., & Miletich, S. (2010, November 22). Videos show Williams' numerous encounters with police. *The Seattle Times.* Retrieved from http://seattletimes.nwsource.com/html/localnews/2013497943_policeshooting23m.html

Cat put in wheelie bin: "Death to Mary Bale" Facebook page taken down. (2010, August 25). *The Telegraph.* Retrieved from http://www.telegraph.co.uk/news/uknews/7963804/Cat-put-in-wheelie-bin-Death-to-Mary-Bale-Facebook-page-taken-down.html

Center for Constitutional Rights. (2010a). *NYPD stop-and-frisk statistics 2009 and 2010.* New York, NY: Author.

Center for Constitutional Rights. (2010b). *Stop-and-frisk: Fagan report summary.* Retrieved from http://ccrjustice.org/files/Fagan%20Report%20Summary%20Final.pdf

Cooper, C. C. (2010, June 23). National Black Police Association (NBPA) statement on the punching of a jaywalker by a Seattle policemen [Editorial]. *The Seattle Medium.* Retrieved from http://www.seattlemedium.com/news

Craig, G. (2011, September 3). Rochester police to learn from Emily Good case. *Democrat and Chronicle.com.* Retrieved from http://www.democratandchronicle.com/article/20110903/NEWS01/109030342/Rochester-police-learn-from-Emily-Good-case

Davis, R. C., Henderson, N. J., & Cheryachukin, Y. (2004). *Assessing police–public contacts in Seattle, WA.* New York, NY: Vera Institute of Justice.

Ehrlich, B. (2010). The ballad of cat bin lady: The Internet's latest viral villain. *Mashable.* Retrieved from http://mashable.com/2010/08/26/cat-bin-lad/

Flanagan, T. J., & Vaughn, M. S. (1996). Public opinion about police use of force. In W. A. Geller & H. Toch (Eds.), *Police violence: Understanding and controlling police abuse of force* (pp. 113–128). New Haven, CT: Yale University Press.

Floyd v. City of New York, 08 Civ. 1034 (SAS 2008).

The Gain mutiny. (1971, December 27). *Newsweek, 35.*

Glik v. Cunniffe, 2011 WL 3769092 (C.A.1 [Mass.]).

Goffman, E. (1959). *The presentation of self in everyday life.* New York, NY: Doubleday.

Goldstein, H. (1987). Toward community-oriented policing: Potential, basic requirements, and threshold questions. *Crime and Delinquency, 33,* 6–13.

Goldstein, H. (1990). *Problem-oriented policing.* New York, NY: McGraw-Hill.

Green, S. J., & Miletich, S. (2010, September 1). Seattle police have questions about fatal shooting by officer. *The Seattle Times.* Retrieved from http://seattletimes.nwsource.com/html/localnews/2012769201_copshooting01m.html

Groves, W. E. (1968). Police in the ghetto. In P. H. Rossi, R. A. Berk, D. P. Boesel, B. K. Eidson, & W. E. Groves (Eds.), *Between White and Black: The faces of American institutions in the ghetto.* Washington, DC: U.S. Government Printing Office.

Haeck, T. (2010, September 16). Activists demand change within police department. *MyNorthwest.com.* Retrieved from http://mynorthwest.com/category/local_news_articles/20100916/Activists-demand-change-within-police-department/

Heffter, E. (2010, September 23). Some urge expanded civilian role on Seattle police-shooting-review board. *The Seattle Times.* Retrieved from http://seattletimes.nwsource.com/html/localnews/2012981850_firearmsreview24m.html

Herbert, B. (2010, February 2). Jim Crow policing. *The New York Times,* p. A27.

Herbert, B. (2010, July 6). An easy call. *The New York Times,* p. A23.

Herbert, S. (2006). *Citizens, cops, and power: Recognizing the limits of community.* Chicago, IL: University of Chicago Press.

Hundreds rally in Seattle for man shot by police. (2010, September 16). *MyNorthwest.com.* Retrieved from http://www.mynorthwest.com/category/local_news_articles/20100916/Hundreds-rally-in-Seattle-for-man-shot-by-police/

Illinois v. Wardlow, 528 U.S. 119, 120 S.Ct. 673 (2000).

Kelman, H. C. (1958). Compliance, identification, and internalization: Three processes of attitude change. *The Journal of Conflict Resolution, 2,* 51–60. doi:10.1177/002200275800200106

Kerlikowske, R. G. (2001). *SPD special report: Addressing the issue of racial profiling— One year later.* Seattle, WA: Seattle Police Department.

Kerlikowske, R. G. (2007). Message from the chief. In Seattle Police Department (Ed.), *Perspectives: Seattle Police Department annual report* (p. 2). Seattle, WA: Seattle Police Department.

Kimbrough, J. D. (2011, July 26). Re: I agree with the arrest of Emily Good! She should of [sic] listened [Facebook page comment]. Retrieved from http://www. facebook.com/pages/I-Agree-with-the-arrest-of-emily-good-she-should-of-Listened/163963840339333?sk=wall

Kirkwood, G. M. (1954). The dramatic role of the chorus in Sophocles. *The Phoenix, 8,* 1–22.

Large, J. (2011, January 26). Seattle police officer, it's time to turn in the badge. *The Seattle Times.* Retrieved from http://seattletimes.nwsource.com/html/jerrylarge/2014048796_jdl27.html

Lewin, K. (1947). Group decision and social change. In T. M. Newcomb & E. L. Hartley, (Eds.), *Readings in social psychology* (pp. 330–344). New York, NY: Holt.

Lingering questions about "stop-and-frisk" [Editorial]. (2010, February 18). *The New York Times,* p. A26.

Locke, H. G. (1996). The color of law and the issue of color: Race and the abuse of police power. In W. A. Geller & H. Toch (Eds.), *Police violence: Understanding and controlling police abuse of force* (pp. 129–149). New Haven, CT: Yale University Press.

Lyons, W. (1999). *The politics of community policing: Rearranging the power to punish.* Ann Arbor: University of Michigan Press.

Maclin, T. (1998). Terry v. Ohio's Fourth Amendment legacy: Black men and police discretion. *St. John's Law Review, 72,* 1271–1322.

Madrid, C. (2010, September 3). Candlelight vigil commemorates life of John T. Williams. *The Stranger.* Retrieved from http://slog.thestranger.com/slog/archives/2010/09/03/candlelight-vigil-commemorates-life-of-shooting-victim

Madrid, C. (2011, January 27). Chief Diaz takes more active leadership role at local crime meeting. *The Stranger.* Retrieved from http://slog.thestranger.com/slog/archives/2011/01/27/chief-diaz-steps-out-condemns-guardian-articles-takes-responsibility-for-spd-at-local-crime-meeting

Manning, P. K. (1977). *Police work: The social organization of policing.* Cambridge, MA: MIT Press.

Manning, P. K. (2003). *Policing contingencies.* Chicago, IL: University of Chicago Press.

Mapes, L. V. (2010, September 17). Mayor meets with protesters over carver's fatal shooting. *The Seattle Times.* Retrieved from http://seattletimes.nwsource.com/html/localnews/2012920846_march17m.html

Maria. (2004, February 9). Greek/Choir role in theater: Answer. *AllExperts.* Retrieved from http://en.allexperts.com/q/Greek-2004/Choir-role-theater.htm

Martinez, E. (2010, June 18). Poll: Cop punches woman (VIDEO), justified or police brutality? *Crimesider*. Retrieved from http://www.cbsnews.com/8301-504083_162-20008175-504083.html?tag=mncol;lst;1

McElroy, W. (2010). Are cameras the new guns? *Gizmodo*. Retrieved from http://gizmodo.com/5553765

McGinn, M. (2011, February 16). *Statement on Officer Birk's resignation* [News Release]. Retrieved from http://mayormcginn.seattle.gov/statement-on-officer-birks-resignation/

McNerthney, C. (2010, June 14). Police Guild: Officer did nothing wrong in video punch. *Seattle pi*. Retrieved from http://www.seattlepi.com/default/article/Police-guild-Officer-did-nothing-wrong-in-885514.php

McNerthney, C. (2010, June 17). Police union response to City Attorney slam for jaywalking punch. *Seattle 911*. Retrieved from http://blog.seattlepi.com/seattle911/2010/06/17/police-union-response-to-city-attorney-slam-for-jaywalking-punch/

McNerthney, C. (2010, September 22). Police detail force training, racial profiling training. *Seattle pi*. Retrieved from http://www.seattlepi.com/default/article/Police-detail-force-training-racial-profiling-889067.php

McNerthney, C., & Gutierrez, S. (2010, October 14). Report: Police shooting of woodcarver not justified. *Seattle pi*. Retrieved from http://www.seattlepi.com/default/article/Report-Police-shooting-of-woodcarver-not-890075.php

Miletich, S. (2010, June 16). Auditors have cited concerns with Seattle police jaywalking stops. *The Seattle Times*. Retrieved from http://seattletimes.nwsource.com/html/localnews/2012136804_coppunch17m.html

Miletich, S. (2010, November 23). Seattle police might ask State Patrol to examine officer's kicking of suspect. *The Seattle Times*. Retrieved from http://seattletimes.nwsource.com/html/localnews/2013507380_policevideo24m.html

Miletich, S. (2010, December 7a). SPD officer who punched teen in jaywalking incident cleared of excessive force. *The Seattle Times*. Retrieved from http://seattletimes.nwsource.com/html/localnews/2013620337_jaywalking08m.html

Miletich, S. (2010, December 7b). State Patrol to launch criminal probe of SPD officer who kicked suspect. *The Seattle Times*. Retrieved from http://seattletimes.nwsource.com/html/localnews/2013619553_copkick08m.html

Miletich, S. (2010, December 17). Police video documents fatal encounter between officer and woodcarver. *The Seattle Times*. Retrieved from http://seattletimes.nwsource.com/html/localnews/2013705989_video18m.html

Miletich, S. (2011, January 9). Inquest into police shooting of woodcarver will answer some questions, but leave tough decisions for others. *The Seattle Times*. Retrieved from http://seattletimes.nwsource.com/html/localnews/2013892533_inquest10m.html

Miletich, S. (2011, February 3). City Hall forum in Seattle police conduct erupts in anger, mistrust. *The Seattle Times*. Retrieved from http://seattletimes.nwsource. com/html/localnews/2014125462_accountability04m.html

Miletich, S., & Clarridge, C. (2011, January 11). Officer on fatal shooting: "No doubt . . . attack was coming." *The Seattle Times*. Retrieved from http:// seattletimes.nwsource.com/html/localnews/2013905500_inquest12m.html

Miletich, S., & Heffter, E. (2010, September 15). Officer's shooting of woodcarver prompts shake-up in Seattle Police Department. *The Seattle Times*. Retrieved from http://seattletimes.nwsource.com/html/localnews/2012903347_police review16m.html

Miletich, S., & Heffter, E. (2010, September 23). Seattle shakes up police command ranks after fatal shooting of woodcarver. *The Seattle Times*. Retrieved from http:// community.seattletimes.nwsource.com/mobile/?type=story&id=2012903347&

Miletich, S., & Sullivan, J. (2010, June 15). Seattle police to review tactics, officer's conduct after videotaped punch. *The Seattle Times*. Retrieved from http://seattle times.nwsource.com/html/localnews/2012122660_coppunch16m.html

Miletich, S., & Sullivan, J. (2010, October 14). Woodcarver's shooting by SPD officer ruled not justified in preliminary finding. *The Seattle Times*. Retrieved from http://seattletimes.nwsource.com/html/localnews/2013160320_shooting 15m.html

Miletich, S., & Sullivan, J. (2010, November 18). Seattle officer's kicking of suspect prompts call for federal civil-rights review. *The Seattle Times*. Retrieved from http://seattletimes.nwsource.com/html/localnews/2013465458_copkick 19m.html

Miletich, S., & Sullivan, J. (2011, January 20). Inquest jurors split over Seattle police shooting. *The Seattle Times*. Retrieved from http://seattletimes.nwsource. com/html/localnews/2013989423_inquest21m.html

Miletich, S., & Sullivan, J. (2011, January 20). Inquest jury: Williams didn't have time to drop knife. *The Seattle* Times. Retrieved from http://seattletimes. nwsource.com/ABPub/zoom/html/2013990550.html

Miletich, S., & Sullivan, J. (2011, February 16). Officer Birk quits after SPD rebuke. *The Seattle Times*. Retrieved from http://seattletimes.nwsource.com/html/ localnews/2014241632_policeshooting17m.html

Milgram, S., & Toch, H. (1969). Collective behavior: Crowds and social movements. In G. Lindzey & E. Aronson (Eds.), *The handbook of social psychology* (2nd ed., pp. 507–610). Reading, MA: Addison-Wesley.

Muir, W. K. (1977). *Police: Streetcorner politicians*. Chicago, IL: University of Chicago Press.

Murphy, K. (2010, September 17). Seattle in turmoil over police-involved shootings: The killing of a Native-American is the latest to prompt scrutiny of rules using force. *The Los Angeles Times*. Retrieved from http://articles.latimes.com

National Advisory Commission on Civil Disorders. (1968). *Report of the National Advisory Commission on Civil Disorders*. Washington, DC: U.S. Government Printing Office.

Obama-like beer summit—minus the beer—for jaywalking teen and South Precinct Officer. (2010, June 18). *Rainier Valley Post*. Retrieved from http://www.rainiervalleypost.com/obama-like-beer-summit-minus-the-beer-for-jaywalking-teen-south-precinct-officer/

O'Donnell, E. (2010, July 3). [Letter to the Editor]. *The New York Times*.

Office of the Mayor. (2010). *Appendix B: Status update on the investigation of the fatal shooting of John T. Williams by a Seattle police officer*. Retrieved from http://www.seattle.gov/mayor/PDF/100915PR-AppxB-investigationStatus Update.pdf

Officers threatened after Emily Good arrest. (2011, July 5). *PoliceOne.com*. Retrieved from http://www.policeone.com/police-products/investigation/evidence-management/articles/3899228-Officers-threatened-after-Emily-Good-arrest/

O'Hagan, M. (2010, June 15). Man who videotaped punch: "In the right spot at the right time." *The Seattle Times*. Retrieved from http://www.seattletimes.nwsource.com/html/localnews/2012126643_videographer16m.html

O'Neill, R. (2011, February). President's message. *The Guardian*, pp. 2–3.

Paul, A. M. (2011, January 31). The roar of the tiger mom. *Time, 26*, pp. 34–40.

Perez, T. E. (2011, March 31). [Letter to the Honorable Michael McGinn]. *The Seattle Times*. Retrieved from http://seattletimes.nwsource.com/ABPub/2011/03/31/2014648498.pdf

Pflaumer, K. (2008, October 8). *Office of Professional Accountability auditor's report on obstruction arrests, January 2006–July 2008*. Seattle, WA: Author.

Pflaumer, K. (2009, March 12). *OPA auditor's report on the Seattle Police Department's relationship with diverse communities*. Seattle, WA: Author.

Pomper, S. (2007). *Is there a problem, officer? A cop's inside scoop on avoiding traffic tickets*. Guilford, CT: Lyons Press.

Pomper, S. (n.d.). *Steve Pomper* [Author biography]. Retrieved from http://www.amazon.com/Steve-Pomper/e/B001JP7K12

President's Commission on Law Enforcement and the Administration of Justice (1967). *The challenge of crime in a free society*. Washington, DC: U.S. Government Printing Office.

Radil, A. (2010, September 17). Civilian observer says Seattle Police Review Board puts her on sidelines. *KUOW.org*. Retrieved from http://www.kuow.org/program.php?id=21401

Radil, A. (2010, September 24). More Tasers at SPD, but that wouldn't have changed John Williams shooting. *KUOW.org*. Retrieved from http://kuow.org/program.php?id=21469

Reiss, A. J. (1971). *The police and the public.* New Haven, CT: Yale University Press.

Reiss, A. J. (1985). Shaping and serving the community: The role of the police executive. In W. A. Geller (Ed.), *Police leadership in America: Crisis and opportunity* (pp. 61–70). New York, NY: Praeger.

ridoshi2117. (2011, June 25). *Emily Good discusses arrest by Rochester Police* [Video file]. Retrieved from http://www.youtube.com/watch?v=3aOUuh9cos0

Rivera, R., Baker, A., & Roberts, J. (2010, July 11). Over four years, nearly 52,000 police stops in a few Brooklyn blocks. *The New York Times,* pp. A1, A17.

Romero, R., & Forman, J. (2010, June 15). Police, community respond to video of SPD officer punching teen. *King5.com.* Retrieved from http://www.king5.com/news/home/Seattle-police-respond-to-videotape-of-officer-punching-woman-96403019.html

Sadd, S., & Grinc, R. M. (1996). *Implementation challenges in community policing: Innovative neighborhood-oriented policing in eight cities.* Washington, DC: National Institute of Justice.

Scenario. (1984). In *The Merriam-Webster Dictionary* (9th ed.). Springfield, MA: Merriam-Webster.

Seattle City Council. (2006, February 23). *Citizen member sought for firearms review board.* Retrieved from http://www.seattle.gov/council/newsdetail.asp?ID=5905&Dept=28

Seattle jaywalkers unite. (2003, August 11). *tqed.com: y'all can't all be wrong.* Retrieved from http://web.archive.org/web/20041025212108/http://tqed.com/archives/000081.jsp

Seattle PD investigates cop who kicked teen. (2010, November 18). *PoliceOne.com.* Retrieved from http://www.policeone.com/officer-misconduct-internal-affairs/articles/2920332-Video-Seattle-PD-investigates-cop-who-kicked-teen/

Seattle Police Chief Diaz reorganizes command structure. (2010, September 21). *West Seattle Herald.* Retrieved from http://www.westseattleherald.com/2010/09/15/news/seattle-police-chief-diaz-reorganizes-command-str

Seattle Police Department. (2002, July 22). Department mission statement and priorities. *Policies and procedures* (Section 1.040). Retrieved from http://www.seattle.gov/police/publications/Policy/SPD_Manual.pdf

Seattle Police Department. (2004). Unbiased policing. *Policies and procedures* (Section 1.010). Retrieved from http://www.seattle.gov/police/publications/Policy/SPD_Manual.pdf

Seattle Police Department. (2008). Citizen observation of officers. *Policies and procedures* (Section 17.070). Retrieved from http://www.seattle.gov/police/publications/Policy/SPD_Manual.pdf

Seattle Police Department. (2010). Firearms Review Board process. *Policies and procedures* (Section 1.305). Retrieved from http://www.seattle.gov/police

Seattle Police Department. (2011, February 16). Statement of Police Chief John Diaz. *SPD Blotter*. Retrieved from http://spdblotter.seattle.gov/2011/02/16/statement-of-police-chief-john-diaz/

Seattle police look into officer's use of force during arrest. (2010, November 18). *KATU.com*. Retrieved from http://www.katu.com/news/local/108958634.html

Seattle police officers: A call for accountability [Editorial]. (2011, February 4). *The Seattle Times*. Retrieved from http://seattletimes.nwsource.com/html/editorials/2014134477_edit05police.html

Seattle police union defends officer in last video. (2010, November 18). *q13fox.com*. Retrieved from http://www.q13fox.com/news/kcpq-seattle-police-union-defends-o-111810,0,610627.story

Seelye, K. Q. (2011, July 29). Twitter as police scanner draws feedback in Seattle. *New York Times*, p. A17.

Sheridan, M. (2010, August 25). Mary Bale, caught on video throwing cat into trash bin, says "sorry" after receiving death threats. *NYDailyNews.com*. Retrieved from http://www.nydailynews.com/news/world/2010/08/25/2010-08-25_mary_bale_caught_on_video_throwing_cat_into_trash_bin_says_sorry_after_death_thr.html

Sibron v. State of New York, Peters v. State of New York, 392 U.S. 40, 88 S.Ct. 1889 (1968).

Skogan, W. G. (2008). Why reforms fail. *Policing and Society, 18,* 23–34. doi:10.1080/10439460701718534

Sledge, M. (2011, June 22). Rochester woman arrested after videotaping police from her own front yard. *The Huffington Post*. Retrieved from http://www.huffingtonpost.com/2011/06/22/emily-good-arrested-videotaping-police-rochester_n_882122.html

Snead, E. (2010, August 25). Mary Bale: "Funny" to put cat in garbage, death threats not so funny. *Zap2it*. Retrieved from http://blog.zap2it.com/pop2it/2010/08/mary-bale-funny-to-put-cat-in-garbage-death-threats-not-so-funny.html#top-comment-nav

Stoltz, A. (2011, February 20). No room for even one? *The Guardian*, p. 4.

Sullivan, J. (2011, January 19). Update: Inquest jury to resume deliberations Thursday. *The Seattle Times*. Retrieved from http://seattletimes.nwsource.com/html/theblotter/2013975733_list_of_questions_being_delibe.html

Task Force on the Police, President's Commission on Law Enforcement and Administration of Justice. (1967). *Task force: The police*. Washington, DC: U.S. Government Printing Office.

Terry v. State of Ohio, 392 U.S. 1, 88 S.Ct. 1868 (1968).

Thomas, L. (2011, March 28). SPD officer's view of socialist Seattle. *MYNorthwest.com*. Retrieved from http://www.mynorthwest.com/?nid=646&sid=416027

Toch, H. (1969). *Violent men: An inquiry into the psychology of violence.* Chicago, IL: Aldine.

Toch, H., & Grant, J. D. (2005). *Police as problem solvers: How frontline workers can promote organizational and community change* (2nd ed.). Washington, DC: American Psychological Association.

Toch, H., Grant, J. D., & Galvin, R. T. (1975). *Agents of change: A study in police reform.* Cambridge, MA: Schenkman Books.

Tonry, M. (2011). Less imprisonment is no doubt a good thing. More policing is not. *Criminology & Public Policy, 10,* 137–152. doi:10.1111/j.1745-9133.2010.00692.x

Trowbridge, L. (2010, August 28). U.K. cat-dumping woman may now lose her bank job due to outcry. *Digital Journal.* Retrieved from http://www.digitaljournal.com/article/296709

United States v. Arvizu, 534 U.S. 266 (2002).

Video appears to show second confrontation with suspended Seattle cop. (2010, November 19). *KOMOnews.com.* Retrieved from http://www.komonews.com/news/local/109069539.html

Vila, B., & Morris, C. (Eds.). (1999). *The role of police in American society: A documentary history.* Westport, CT: Greenwood Press.

Walker, S. (1998). *Popular justice: A history of American criminal justice* (2nd ed.). New York, NY: Oxford University Press.

Walker, S. (2005). *The new world of police accountability.* Thousand Oaks, CA: Sage.

Watt, L. M. (1908). *The chorus.* Retrieved from http://www.theatrehistory.com/ancient/chorus001.html

Weitzer, R., & Tuch, S. (2004). *Rethinking minority attitudes toward the police* (Final Technical Report, Grant No. 2001-IJ-CX0016). Washington, DC: National Institute of Justice.

Weitzer, R., & Tuch, S. (2006). *Race and policing in America: Conflict and reform.* New York, NY: Cambridge University Press. doi:10.1017/CBO9780511617256

Wicker, T. (1968). Introduction. In U.S. Riot Commission, *Report of the National Advisory Commission on Civil Disorders* (pp. v–xi). New York, NY: Bantam Books.

The Williams case needs a tangible resolution. (2011, January 21). *The Seattle Times.* Retrieved from http://seattletimes.nwsource.com/html/editorials/2014000924_edit22inquest.html

The Williams shooting: Decertify the law officer [Editorial]. (2011, February 17). *The Seattle Times*. Retrieved from http://seattletimes.nwsource.com/html/editorials/2014259788_edit18birk.html

Workman, D. (2010, October 14). "Unjustified shooting" report good cause for reflection by police, gun activists. *Examiner.com*. Retrieved from http://www.examiner.com/gun-rights-in-seattle/unjustified-shooting-report-good-reason-for-reflection-by-police-gun-activist

Yardley, W. (2011, April 1). Justice Department to review Seattle Police's use of force. *The New York Times*, p. A17.

Index

Broken windows approach, 81
Brownsville, Brooklyn, 162
Bryant, A., 137
Burglars, fleeing, 70
Bystanders. *See also* Spectators
    defined, 5
    obstruction by, 104
    as trespassers, 103

Cameras, 84–85
Carter, M., 125
Catalytic interventions, 7–8
Causation, 10
Cause, probable, 154–155
Cell phones, 5n1
Center for Constitutional Rights, 158
Centralization of power, 72
Change. *See also* Police reform
    agents of, 71–73
    bottom-up, 140–143
    crowds as instigators of, 144
    police culture's support of, 142
    resistance to, 79
    in roles, 100
    top-down, 58–59, 140–143
Cheryachukin, Y., 100–101
Chorus concept, 4–5, 82–89
Citizens, 104, 116–117
Citizenship programs, 78
Civil rights, 46, 108
Clamorous chorus, 88
Clarridge, C., 127–128
Collective resentment, 6
Community-oriented policing, 77–90
    advent of, 77–80
    development of, 142–143
    and media attention, 82–86
    and network formation, 86–89
    as officer-oriented, 141–143
    outreach in, 112–113
    in police reform, 89–90
    and quality of life problems,
        80–82

and resentment, 98–100
    in Seattle police department,
        137–138
Community-relations reforms, 57–73
    citizen complaints in, 69–71
    crime suppression in, 60–61
    minority officers in, 64–67
    objectives of, 59
    police leadership in, 71–73
    police misconduct in, 67–69
    police resistance to, 57–59
    police training in, 61–64
    social work in, 60–61
Competing mutual support, 26–30
Complaints
    about profiling, 162–163
    anonymous, 69–71
    in community-relations reforms,
        69–71
COMPuter STATistics/COMParative
        STATistics (COMPSTAT),
        148n2
Computer technology, 84, 148n2
Confidence, 9, 10
Conflict, physical. *See* Physical con-
        frontation
Control, preventive aggressive, 148
Co-optation, 40–44
Crime statistics, 102–103
Crime suppression, 60–61, 81–82
Crisis intervention training, 113–114
Crowd formation, 85–86
Crowd psychology, 6–7, 144
Cultural sensitivity
    and due process, 138–140
    and minority neighborhoods,
        39–40, 61–62
    in police reform, 109–111
Curriculum, 62–63
Custer's Last Stand, 47

Davis, R. C., 100–101
Davis, R. L., 151

power of, 143–144
and racial bias, 136
on videotaped encounters, 84–86,
95–96
Public relations
goals in, 100
and police reform, 12–13
police union campaigns of, 133

Quality of life, 80–82

Race. *See also* Profiling
in jaywalking incident, 95–96
in 1960s police encounters, 49–51
in police shootings, 120–121
in precipitation of riots, 8–11
and public opinion, 136
stereotypes of, 162
in stop-and-frisk procedures,
148–149, 158
in volatile scenarios, 150–152
Race and social-justice training,
138–143
Real-world scenarios, 18, 20–21
Reasonable suspicion
and policing experience, 161–162
Supreme Court rulings on,
153–154, 161
in volatile scenarios, 158–159
Reconciliation events, 97–98
Recruitment, 64–67
Recruit training. *See* Police training
Rehnquist, William, 159–161
Reiss, A. J., 8, 12, 79
Relationship building, 98–100
Resentment
about jaywalking laws, 106–107
collective, 6
in minority neighborhoods, 71,
100–101
in police departments, 77–78
reduction in, 98–100

Resistance
to community relations training,
61–64
to internal investigation, 67–70
to minority officer recruitment,
64–67
to police authority, 8–10
to police reform, 57–61, 71–73
to role changes, 100
Right to counsel, 152
Riots
causation of, 10
and crowd formation, 7
Kerner Commission on, 9
and physical force, 35–36
police precipitation of, 8–11, 13
and poverty, 13n3
and "professionalism" of officers,
6, 148
Watts, 10, 13n3
Risk, 84
Rivera, R., 162
Roberts, J., 162
Root, O., 151

Sadd, S., 142
Scapegoating, 49
Scenarios, 17–20
Search warrants, 152
Seattle incident, 131–132
Seattle Police Department, 120
and attack on teenage girl, 91–93
community relations efforts of, 99
concerns addressed by, 101
counterpart announcement of, 97
critiques of, 96
and due process, 137–144
FRB, 116–118
internal review entity of, 101
and racial percentages in arrests,
102–103
as target of community-oriented
reform, 89–90

About the Author

Hans Toch, PhD, is distinguished professor emeritus at the University of Albany at the State University of New York, where he is affiliated with the School of Criminal Justice. He obtained his PhD in social psychology at Princeton University, has taught at Michigan State University and at Harvard University, and, in 1996, served as the Walker-Ames Professor at the University of Washington, Seattle. He is a fellow of both the American Psychological Association and the American Society of Criminology. In 1996, he acted as president of the American Association of Correctional Psychology. He is a recipient of the Hadley Cantril Memorial Award (for *Men in Crisis: Human Breakdowns in Prison*), the August Vollmer Award of the American Society of Criminology for outstanding contributions to applied criminology, the Prix deGreff from the International Society of Criminology for Distinction in Clinical Criminology, and the Research Award of the International Corrections and Prison Association.

His research interests range from mental health problems and the psychology of violence to issues of organizational reform and planned change. His books include *Violent Men: An Inquiry Into the Psychology of Violence* (1992), *Living in Prison: The Ecology of Survival* (1992), *Mosaic of Despair: Human Breakdowns in Prison* (1992), *The Disturbed Violent Offender* (with Kenneth Adams, 1994), *Police Violence: Understanding and Controlling Police Abuse of Force* (with William Geller, 1996), *Corrections: A Humanistic Approach* (1997), *Crime and Punishment: Inside Views* (with

Robert Johnson, 2000), *Acting Out: Maladapive Behavior in Confinement* (with Kenneth Adams, 2002), *Stress in Policing* (2002), and *Police as Problem Solvers: How Frontline Workers Can Promote Organizational and Community Change* (2005).